All My Friends Are Rock Stars

The music scenes of Rockford IL, Madison & Milwaukee WI; 80's and 90's.

Written & Edited by Theron Moore
Interviews conducted by Theron Moore

Mean Machine Press © 2015

Theronmoore1@gmail.com

Cover Model: Mareya Gutierrez

Printing History: Print Version, 2015, First Edition

The **STARS** of this book in order of appearance:

Bun E. Carlos / Cheap Trick
Mark Snodgrass / *"Listen To This"* Radio Show
Greg / Pure Aggression
Brian Carter / Sarkoma
Glenn Rene Zeringue Junior / Bludgeoned Nun
Dan Gildea / Pinewood Box
Dave Ensminger / Pinewood Box
A Short History of Punk and Indie Rock in Rockford, Illinois
Jerry Sofran / forchristsake / Rude Awakening
Ray Horstheimer/ Bugzy Malone
Paul Bronson / Zanthus
Dave Potter / Music & Program Director of Y95
Midwest Jamfest
Todd Houston / Midnite Angel
Greg DeCarlo / RIPT
Steve Moriarty / RIPT
Mike Korn / RAM Magazine
Author Commentary Madison and Milwaukee
Brad Skaife / Imminent Attack
Biff Blumfumgagnge / The Gomers
Bill Feeny / Appliances S.F.B.
Dan Hobson / Killdozer
Mike Turnis / Horny Genius
Blunt Rapture / Cattle Prod & Headpump
Bucky Pope / Tar Babies
O'Cayz Corral
Robert Corbitt
Cathy Dethmers / O'Cayz Corral
Paul Schluter / Last Crack
Dave Gregor / Morta Skuld
Rich Noonan / Dr. Shrinker
Jackie Ramos / Moxy Roxx
Greg Kalember / Raven Bitch
Morgan Thorn / Megaton Blonde
Jack Koshick / Concert Promoter

Table of Contents:

Origins; **Pages 11-17**

Bun E. Carlos / Cheap Trick; **Pages 19-22**

Mark Snodgrass / "*Listen To This*" Radio Show; **Pages 23-35**

Greg / Pure Aggression; **Pages 36-49**

Brian Carter / Sarkoma; **Pages 50-57**

Glenn Rene Zeringue Junior / Bludgeoned Nun; **Pages 58-64**

Dan Gildea / Pinewood Box; **Pages 65-71**

Dave Ensminger / Pinewood Box; **Pages 72-82**

A Short History of Punk / Indie Rock in Rockford; **Pages 83-86**

Jerry Sofran / forchristsake / Rude Awakening; **Pages 87-100**

Ray Horstheimer / Bugzy Malone; **Pages 101-111**

Paul Bronson / Zanthus; **Pages 112-116**

Dave Potter / Music & Program Director of Y95; **Pages 117-123**

Midwest Jamfest; **Pages 124-136**

Todd Houston / Midnite Angel; **Pages 137-143**

Greg DeCarlo / RIPT; **Pages 144-150**

Steve Moriarty / RIPT; **Pages 151-155**

Mike Korn / RAM Magazine; **Pages 156-164**

Madison and Milwaukee; **Pages 165-170**

Brad Skaife / Imminent Attack; **Pages 171-186**

Biff Blumfumgagnge / The Gomers; **Pages 187-192**

Bill Feeny / Appliances S.F.B., **Pages 193-203**

Dan Hobson / Killdozer; **Pages 204-211**

Mike Turnis / Horny Genius; **Pages 212-220**

Blunt Rapture / Cattle Prod; **Pages 221-227**

Frank "Bucky" Pope / Tar Babies; **Pages 228-231**

O'Cayz Corral; Pages 232-249

Robert Corbitt; **Pages 235-242**

Cathy Dethmers / O'Cayz Corral; **Pages 243-250**

Paul Schluter / Last Crack; **Pages 251-268**

Dave Gregor / Morta Skuld; **Pages 269-275**

Rich Noonan / Dr. Shrinker; **Pages 276-285**

Jackie Ramos / Moxy Roxx; **Pages 286-298**

Greg Kalember / Raven Bitch; **Pages 299-307**

Morgan Thorn / Megaton Blonde; **Pages 308-320**

Jack Koshick / Concert Promoter; **Pages 321-340**

About the Author; Pages 342

Photo Credits; Pages 342-346

Special Thanks:

Jerry Sofran & Todd Houston -- Thanks for the help and info provided. I owe you shots and beers next time I'm in Rockford…

My wife Jeanette for allowing me to indulge and get this book done. Much love always!

Everyone in this book. Thank you for your time so I could tell your story. It was a fun ride then and still a fun ride now.

                    RUSSELL
          ... and it's okay, because rock and
          roll is a LIFESTYLE... and a way of
          thinking and it's not about money and
          "popularity!"

                    JEFF
          Some money would be nice.

Jeff sprays some shaving cream into his palm, and rubs it into his scalp - poor man's mousse.

                    RUSSELL
          - but it's a voice that says here I
          am... and FUCK YOU if you can't
          understand me.

          From the script "Almost Famous" by Cameron Crow

Origins

I'm at that age, middle age, where I'm mandated by corporate America and the wholly owned subsidiaries thereof, to listen to Blake Shelton and whatever's VH1 or VH1 Classic-friendly, spending weekends using power tools in my neatly organized garage or doing yard work per the rules of adulthood and suburbia. Only problem is, I can't get behind that.

I still like a good, stiff drink. I still listen to hard rock and metal. I still love punk and grindcore and I still dig the underground and all it stands for. To me that's living; it's dynamic, it's happening, it's NOW. I used to do a print zine called *"Louder Than God"* back in the 80's / 90's – metal, punk, local bands, you name it, I covered it. Whatever got me off I wrote about it.

Present day, 2015 and not much has changed except the format and name of what I'm doing, namely my blog the *"Church of the Necronomicon."* Death, doom, thrash, punk, film, it's all there. Once writing gets under your skin it never leaves. Just like music.

26 years later I'm still freelance writing and self-publishing. Today I'm married with a family, but they get me, thank god. They tolerate my music and my creative endeavors, like this book, which has been gestating inside me since 2011.

It dawned on me I should do it, write about the music scenes I grew up with in Rockford, Madison and to a lesser extent, Milwaukee. Document it. Get it down on paper. Those times were exciting, the bands were great and a lot of 'em became good friends of mine over the years. But doing this book is also closure for me to a certain extent. I left Northern Illinois for a four-year stint in the Air Force. Good or bad I did it. 1992. When I left, the scene was on fire in Rockford. Things were happening. So doing this book, it feels good, and the timing of this project feels right as well.

So I began writing "All My Friends…" on and off, 2011. I'd stop and start another project, come back to it, get derailed by the usual life "stuff" that comes up but in the last ten months I threw myself into this, wanting to get this done, get it published. I still feel a connection back home. These bands, these scenes, they need to be talked about. My job as a writer and editor for this book is to not just interview a band but to tell their story, allow their voices to be heard.

I don't expect to make the NY Times bestseller list and I'm OK with that. I just want a document that people can read and refer to that's a showcase for this snapshot in time when rock N roll was alive and well, when we were all kids and music was the gasoline that fueled us. And through it all, good and bad, great music and scenes were created. I'm no expert just a fan. And the time is right to revisit the past asking one simple question:

"Looking back on the music scene of the 80's and / or 90's, was it as strong and dynamic as you remember it?"

That's how the conversation starts, with this one question, and everything else builds around it. That's what I wanted to know because we're stuffy adults now, moms and dads, teachers, engineers, etc. How do we recollect on these memories, all those years ago?

With the advent of social networking, especially Facebook, I reached out to a lot of people I haven't spoken to in years or even decades and talked about this with them. Some got back to me and some didn't. Some participated and some didn't. That's fine. We're all busy people and in the end I'm still a fan regardless, always will be.

Appetite for Creation

So the more I wrote and did interviews and explored this topic the more it made me wonder why we do what we do from a creative standpoint. Why form bands? Why write? Why create? We did and still do.

The bands I cover in this book, most of them never made it rich off the rock star trip but they held to it, stayed true. And a lot of 'em still play to this day, for what? Not for wealth or fortune.

Success in art is measured differently than success elsewhere, especially in the business world. Although we'd like the culmination of our efforts to be reflected in a few bucks here and there it's actually gauged by the creative community we're affiliated with, the friendships we form, the connections we make, the output we produce.

I believe that as an artist we feed each other's appetite, fan and band alike, each other's inner beast that needs to be exorcised and entertained creatively, powered by the primal energy of youth and excitement that begs not to be restrained.

We write, drink, perform, fuck and repeat again because we have to, we love it, we're connected to it. It's who we are, what's inside us, what moves us forward, even keeps us alive.

Somehow we reach out and connect with each other on common ground with shared purpose, in this case, the music scenes of Rockford, Madison and Milwaukee mid-80's / mid-90's. We all came together. That's what a *good* scene does or should do. That's why a *good* scene is remembered and wrote about years later, hence now.

About the Author

Music and writing have always been my passion. I began writing for *SLAM* Magazine (*State Line Area Magazine*) in the summer of 1988, right around the time I met Mark Snodgrass who produced the state line radio show "*Listen To This*." He was a manager at Little Caesars Pizza in Belvidere, the same joint my brother worked at. It was a lot of drinking, hanging out, fun times. To this day Mark is a close, close friend of mine.

SLAM was a wild experience for me. Up until this point I was just a young metal kid who watched *"Headbanger's Ball"* and read *"Hit Parader Magazine,"* all pre-internet.

Thanks to *SLAM*, I was talking to rock stars on the phone. It was an oddball marriage of the real and the surreal. Often times my parents would answer the phone and I'd hear, *"Hey Theron, Bruce from Rigor Mortis is calling you, please take it..."* or the time my dad spoke to Glen Benton from *Deicide* when I wasn't home to take the call. My dad was like, *"Wow he's really intense and he has a really, really deep voice, who is this guy?"* I even got into Alpine Valley to see Hericane Alice, Bad English, Skid Row, Great White and Whitesnake thks to *SLAM* with a little help from Budweiser as well...

I spoke to bands, communicated with record labels, received free swag and got into MANY a rock concert, always backstage and on the guest list. About a year later the paper went through a major editorial / ideological shift and I left. Or I was let go. I guess it's a *Vince Neil* type thing, depending on who you talk to.

I started a zine called "*Louder than God!*" named after the *Blue Cheer* record of the same name. I focused on death metal, thrash and punk rock while elusively chasing any member, former or not, of *Blue Cheer*.

What I took with me post SLAM was their appreciation for local music which is how I initially met RIPT and Mirrored Image (later forchristsake). I interviewed RIPT at the A-Frame restaurant in Rockford over many, many pitchers of beer.

I saw Mirrored Image at The Cherry Lounge in one of their last shows under that moniker. It was bassist Jerry Sofran who invited me over to the house to do the interview. I was there several times after that and always blown away by how kind and down to Earth those guys were, hell, still are.

On one of the last occasions I had hanging out with forchristsake was the weekend Vancouver band *Caustic Thought* was in town. Not only did I interview them but they took me to a rehearsal space on 7th street they were using and performed several songs live for me.

There were two guys in *Caustic Thought* who found future success with bands such as *Strapping Young Lad, Fear*

Factory, The Devin Townsend band, Zimmers Hole and *Three Inches of Blood*. One was Devin Townsend, the other was Byron Stroud. Nicest guys you'd ever meet.

I met Greg C. from the band Pure Aggression in the winter / spring of '91 / '92 through Mark Snodgrass. Mark introduced me to them and the rest is history. Today Mark and Greg are still friends of mine although we all live hundreds of miles apart.

I made the decision to join the USAF in '92 at what might've been the peak of the Rockford hard rock / metal scene. It was a good life move for me. I continued writing, left the military in '96 and relocated to Albuquerque New Mexico.

And here I am, all these years later, trying to make sense of it all. Why, you ask? Because I loved that scene and the people in it. It was a good thing. The scene was done right back then. That's how it should be now.

ROCKFORD, ILLINOIS

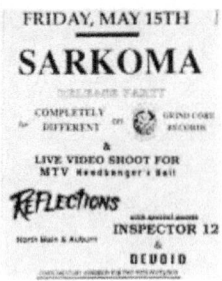

Bun E. Carlos
Cheap Trick

Cheap Trick is blue collar rock N roll at its finest that embraced the Midwestern work ethic of *"hard work pays off"* and it did and Trick connected with the good folk of Northern Illinois who could relate to that.

It wasn't just the music we loved but the connection we had with the band and vice versa. They weren't afraid to be seen in public and mingle with their fans. They were always very visible around the Rockford area.

And all these years later, at age 64, Bun E. Carlos is still that hard working Midwestern rocker who embodies all of this and more.

I remember my first time meeting the band at a local McDonalds I worked at when they stopped in for dinner before heading to Poplar Creek Music Theatre outside of Chicago to open for Motley Crue on their *"Theatre of Pain"* tour and before they left they passed out free tickets to those of us who could go.

Although he isn't touring with Trick he's still the hardest working man in rock today. His side bands include The Bun E. Carlos Experience, The Monday Night Band, Tinted Windows, Candy Golde not to mention a brief reunion with pre-CT band "The Pagans" (1966 to 1968).

He's also the chief archivist of Trick history and a walking rock N roll encyclopedia and if I haven't mentioned it yet, he's one of the coolest, nicest guys you'll ever talk to. This is Bun E. Carlos.

In terms of playing gigs and attending rock shows in Rockford and Northern IL in general, when was it most fun for you? When you were established with Cheap Trick, when you were a kid or chasing the dream of a record deal?

Bun E. Carlos: *Concerts were always fun to attend. Chasing the dream was fun and work.*

As a kid / young man in the 60's and 70's, what were the standout concerts that you attended in Rockford or Northern IL and where were they?

Byrds at Rockford College, Yardbirds at the Rock River Roller Palace, Cream in Beloit, Beatles, Stones, DC5, Who, Hendrix in Chicago.

What about Forest Hills Lodge, I bet you saw quite a few shows there. Did you catch the MC5 show by chance? Which bands do you remember seeing?

I didn't see MC5, had a college class that night. I did see Lovin' Spoonful, The Vogues, lots of local bands at Sherwood Lodge.

What were some of your favorite venues to see shows at in the 60's and 70's in Rockford?

Harlem High School, Rockford College, Ice Chalet.

There were big time rock acts getting booked at Rock Valley College and local high schools back in the 70's. Did you attend a lot any of those shows back then or did Cheap Trick keep you pretty busy?

I saw Delaney and Bonnie at RVC with Mitch Ryder and Billie Preston, otherwise didn't see many school gigs.

If you did show up to a concert were you in the crowd hanging out or watching the gig from side of the stage?

Always looking for the best line of sight.

What local gigs did Cheap Trick do in Rockford or Northern IL in general that standout in your mind as memorable and why?

CT did gigs at over 50 local venues, when I counted them 10 years ago. Northwest Community Center was fun.

Did you see the Ramones when they came to Rockford for the first time, in what, 1979? Had you heard of them at that time?

I saw The Ramones *in 1977 with* The Nerves *opening at The Purchase on Main Street. Both bands were good, I was familiar with both bands.*

Is the local Rockford rock scene still vibrant now or how would you characterize it?

Slowly fading…….

What's the future of rock N roll in Rockford? Do you think the city's economy is a factor?

Like all forms of topical pop music, I think rock is slowly getting older…

Any closing thoughts on local Rockford music you'd like to add?

Rockford's always been a good place to play and has always had a good talent pool of players. As long as the schools teach music that shouldn't change.

Mark Snodgrass
"Listen to This" Radio Show
WLUV

First and foremost, Mark Snodgrass is a good friend. He was a Cali transplant to Rockford IL back in the 80's and became Radio DJ, repo guy, locksmith, band manager for Pure Aggression, you name it and he did it.

Snodgrass played an important role in the 80's rock scene as a radio DJ with his own show in Rockford Illinois.

Mark, you and I played kind of a peripheral role when it came to the Rockford music scene back in the 80's and 90'.

You had a radio show and I did a zine. Tell me about your radio show and how local music figured into it.

Mark Snodgrass: *The show was on WLUV in Loves Park, IL... Serving the greater Rockford area, sometimes down to*

DeKalb when I fiddled with the knobs on the transmitter. What started out as a way for me to get "Alternative" music in front of a major city who only had Top 40, Country and Oldies as their choice at the time, became a major support system for the burgeoning local music scene in the Rockford area.

While being different, eclectic and sounding like pirate radio was the initial draw for attention back when the show started, it was local music that rallied listeners, and support for my little show grew exponentially, as did the local scene now that they had an outlet to be heard by the masses, as opposed to a sweaty basement at the Cherry Lounge.

How did you get that radio gig? What was the day and time you were on the air?

I was a California transplant. I grew up with choices and "alternatives" on the radio. It was natural to me.

So when I landed in Rockford, I was like, what the fuck? Jeff Wicker is a radio "Personality?"

Time and Temp Jocks prevailed, and the music was the same song, at least every hour, with 5 or 6 in regular rotation.

I wanted to hear the stuff Nirvana *was putting out (Prior to Teen Spirit). I wanted to hear* Dead Kennedys, Suicidal Tendencies... *Classic Punk mixed with the new breeds like* The Pixies, *that new band called* Pearl Jam...

No one would touch that shit back then. Grunge was the term for the Mother Love Bone's *and* Screaming Trees

24

and of course Nirvana's *of the day. And I wanted to throw in some twists, like* Tom Waits *and* Leonard Cohen.

I thought what I liked listening to had teeth, had a rhythm that wasn't given a chance to be heard, and should at least be given a chance to be accepted or rejected... rather than being pigeon holed as obscure or to nonconformist. Which ironically is exactly why the local music thing meant so much to me.

No one gave these guys a chance. They were relegated to backrooms and basements. Friend's parties and bootleg cassette tapes. I saw the chance to deliver all of this over the airwaves in the second largest metro area in Illinois... and I took that chance.

Basically, Reader's Digest version of getting the show... I did what I preached from day one on my show. You want to be "punk?" you want to break the rules? You want to cause change and revolt and make a difference? Then do it from within the system.

I got a job at WLUV as a salesman. I worked there for a week, gained the trust of the owner, convinced him Rockford needed a local alternative show to replace the top 40 and sports crap he was satellite shoveling to the masses, and got him to give me a time slot.

I started on Friday nights from 10pm till 2am, pretty quick I got Saturday nights. Then Sundays. Then sporadically through the week... Live remotes n such followed and the thing picked up steam. Called the show "Listen to This."

That station had never been in the ratings, but my timeslots were placing, and on the weekends I was number one.

I was selling actual ads for my show and proved to Joe Salvi (the owner) that I was right. We carried on like that for about two years, till I got too full of myself, thought I could do anything I wanted to do.

The FCC took care of that by suspending me from the airwaves for 6 months following an investigation into reports of foul language and suggestive content.

That's not what they got me for, surprisingly, because there was tons of that going on. What nailed me was not logging commercials.

They require you to mark down that you played a Domino's Pizza spot at, say, 11pm and it ran for 30 sec...Sears had an ad and it ran for 45 seconds, etc...

What I failed to realize was that while I thought I was supporting the local scene, when I said, "Hey – Pure Aggression is playing at Hard Times bar tomorrow night and the doors open at 8pm..." <u>THAT</u> *was a commercial. I just thought I was doing bands and fans a favor.*

Even though I didn't see a penny from that kinda stuff, the FCC saw them as commercials, because someone whether the band or the venue, was cashing in. Joe was in no position to argue with the FCC so he knocked me off the air.

*Quite honestly, he was crying when he told me. And... Quite honestly I was pissed and said fuck radio I'll do something better, I'll do TV. And "*Look at This*" was born.*

After two public access episodes I teamed up with Marc Peabody and landed on WTVO, then NBC. But looking back, I had a face for radio and should have made that my career.

Did you have any local bands on your show?

think I had almost every local band on the show. See, when the story I just exhaustively told began, I was... a security guard. Yeah. Shut up.

*Anyway, one of the guys I worked post with found out about my show, and he's like, "*You gotta hear these guys, maybe put them on your show sometime.*" And proudly handed over a cassette tape of some dudes named* Sarkoma.

I listened to a couple songs, kinda dug 'em and said Fuck it I'll Play it. Never promoted it, never advertised, just put "Dog" on one night while I was doing my show.

I never had the phones light up like they did that night. People were going crazy, fans were calling asking for more. People who didn't know were calling asking who that band was I just played.

I started talking about it on the air. I never knew who they were or what to say about them. Remember, I wasn't from around them parts for long. I played "Holidays" I played "Trolls Opinion" (having no idea what it was about).

The rest of the week was filled with bands calling me to get on the air, notably Pure Aggression, *who played a huge role in my deciding to really pursue and support the local scene. But yeah,* Flac, Sarkoma, Pure Aggression, Shatterd Plastix, Decadenza, DMZ... *A lot of the bands hung around the station, played acoustic sets, helped me torment listeners.*

The station was crazy. My studio was basically a closet with a mixing board and cd players in it and we would cram like 20 people in there, to fit any more we would have needed a lubricant.

And not just bands. I had open invites for listeners to bring by music if they wanted people to hear it and I didn't have it.

Hell, dancers came from State Street Station to party and, um… dance. It was a wild scene, tons of fun. We never planned a night or a show. It just happened

Tell me about the music format you had. I remember hearing punk, metal, etc. on the show.

It was eclectic… I have varied tastes, and I don't think anyone only listens to one type of music, or locks into one genre. A lot of Metal dudes dig Johnny Cash. *Some* Pixies *fans love* Leonard Cohen. *Stu from then* Sarkoma *likes* Tom Waits *and I like it all. So I played it all.*

Kinda like I said above, there was no format. It just happened and evolved at the show went on. Never had a play list, never set a rotation, per se. Only thing I guaranteed was that I wouldn't play the same song twice in a 4 or 6-hour show.

How did you meet Greg from the band Pure Aggression? Was it through the radio show? You were also friends with Sarkoma, correct?

Greg called me shortly after the Sarkoma *thing. Yeah, I used to put my home number out on the air so people could call me and tell me stuff they wanted to hear. So Greg called, and we ended up talking for like 4 or 5 hours.*

He was interested in getting his band, Pure Aggression *on the air, sure. But what struck me was his passion for supporting the local scene. He knew a revolution in radio and local music was on the cusp of blowing up, and he damn well wanted to be part of pushing it over the top.*

Greg is over the top. Anyone who knows him knows he doesn't stop at 110%, He goes all out. I've never seen him do anything half assed or mediocre. After we got off the phone, I knew this guy was gonna be my best friend. And so we were.

He was one of the few who I met through the show that I became friends with because we connected, not because I could get him on the air. Same with the guys from Sarkoma. *Stu, Tony and Brian, especially.*

When I quit the TV show and there was no more looking, or listening or anything to this, they always showed love.

I never really heard much in the years after from most of the bands. Really only Pure Aggression, Sarkoma *and* Decadenza *stuck by me in my normal, non-public life.*

I owe those guys gratitude for not abandoning me in my "Has Been" *years.*

I don't think I've ever asked you this. Were you a thrash or metal fan back then? I know we went to a few PA gigs together, was it just to support Greg and the band?

I liked some metal, but it was Greg who introduced me to the really hardcore stuff.

I went to shows with him and was blown away by the talent those dudes had that others dismissed as noise… and the pure energy and stamina that bled from the stage.

It wasn't until I saw bands like Cannibal Corpse, Demolition Hammer *and of course,* Deicide *live, that I became an honest fan.*

He also turned me on to stuff like Ice T. *I was into old school stuff like* Run DMC *and* Public Enemy *back in the day, but the whole* Ice-T / Body Count *thing was phenomenal. Yeah, I owe that to Greg for broadening my horizons.*

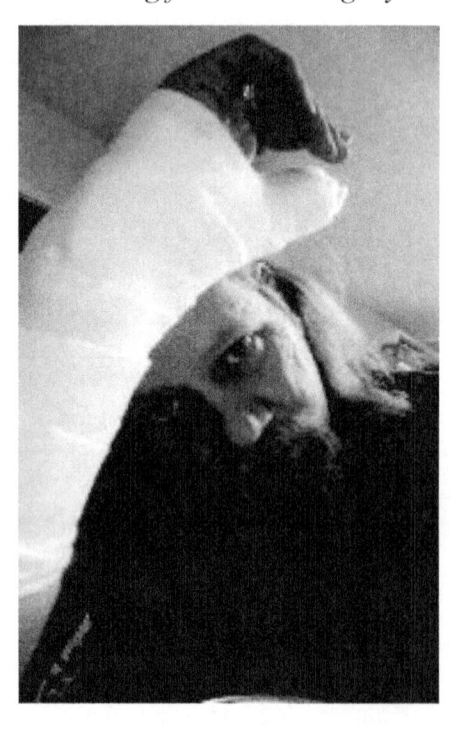

At that point in time when Pure Aggression was active, the Rockford metal scene was thriving. Did you think that maybe Rockford could've been the next big metal scene outside of LA?

I thought Rockford was going to be THE *next big thing. I always said, we're going to be the next Seattle… Not*

just for Metal, not just for Grunge… But the amazing pool of talent that was swimming around back then.
Every Genre really had something special going on. They should have made it… But… it kinda did the Rockford thing and fizzled.

Looking back at that era, what's your opinion now, all these years later? Do you think Rockford could've been the next big metal scene or not?

Could've, yeah… But Rockford could've been a lot of things… and never really was. It's… Rockford.

What circumstances or events needed to have happened back then to have propelled the Rockford music scene into the national spotlight?

Hmmm… I don't want to take blame or credit by saying if I would've kept my head together and my ego intact and found a way to stay on the air, but I've always wondered if that was part of it. Not even me, per se… but some outlet on the airwaves… it would have helped.
Couple other stations and people made valiant, if not misguided attempts at promoting local music, but it was all so… corporate. And never given a chance.
The difference with what I was doing is that I didn't have a station owner or company telling me what to do. The closest thing I had to that was Joe telling me that he heard Fuck go over the air 5 times, and to please knock it off.

Did you promote shows back then? I seem to remember you might've done a Leaving Trains gig? Tell me about that one…

I played a small part in promoting Pure Aggression and Decandenza. *We made this quasi company called "Arsenal Group Productions" with a label of "Mac10 Music" and put together some really cool shows. Um... The Leaving Trains thing... was more of a train wreck.*

They sent this really crazy demand list of perks and such when they were going to come to town.

I flat out told their management I couldn't provide anything of the sort, that I was just a small local dude and was lucky to find them a place to play at. Period. Cancel it, not gonna happen.

Well, their label never told them, it never got through that it wasn't happening. They were totally, understandably, pissed off at me.

They called me for two or three days with threats of... well, tons of bodily harm and shitting into orifices...

Ha, I was pretty freaked out and never booked another touring band gig again

Were you at one point managing Pure Aggression? Tell me about that, was it successful?

In a way, a little. I tried... But I had no idea what we were doing. Gave them some promo ideas, helped set up some shows, like a food drive for the homeless thing at Rock Valley College, but really, Greg was always the boss, it's what he does, the position he puts himself in, because the guy has so much energy and dedication.

What were the circumstances leading up to you disengaging from the Rockford music scene and moving on with your life? At that time I had joined the USAF and was out of town...

After "Listen to This" on the radio, I did the TV thing on NBC called "Look at This." It was cool, and fun and all... Did to TV what I did to Radio.
But after like, a year and a half, I just burned out on TV. It wasn't the same. Radio... it was so... Immediate.
If you did something lame, people called (me out) on it right away. If I did something cool, people called right away. I always had a built in audience, right there in the studio as well.
TV... it was me and sometimes a camera man. And me by myself in the editing room. And I'd work 60 hours a week to film, edit and package a 30 min episode... which I'd get no feedback on for two weeks when it aired.
It was drudgery, and I've never felt comfortable in front of the camera. Not my thing. I was only doing it because no one else did. So I bailed out.
I tried like hell to get back on the radio, but I was kinda black balled in a way. I made enemies of pretty much every station and jock I could make fun of. Ya know, we used to have bonfires at the station, burning other station's stuff.

Listeners would drop off ZOK shirts and WXRX stuff and so forth to win "prizes" (we were low budget, a prize might be a dirty coffee mug with the station owners comb in it, or an old scratched gospel record I found in the AM booth, or a leg bone from a deer the station dog brought back from the corn fields to chew on, stuff like that). We'd make a thing out of burning them every few months.

I mimicked a lot of the other jocks and got kinda good at pissing off pretty much everyone. So going back to radio was outa the question.

So, I went back to the profession I learned while living in Washington DC for a couple years. I went back to repossessing cars. Not much I could do for bands when I was jacking their folk's cars ;)

Where and in what direction did life take you post the Rockford music scene and your involvement with it?

Well, I repossessed cars for years, man. Years. About 7 years ago, my life hit a dead end. Three bouts with cancer and neck vertebrae surgeries, hating my life as a repo man, and a miserable marriage left me depressed, pilled out of my gourd and about to give up.

I had an early midlife crisis and blew my life savings on trips to Europe and cars and pills and... pills. Ha.

I split with my then wife, met my present wife, and she convinced me that in order to be happy and get better, all I needed to do was do what I love. What I was meant to do.

Radio is a very close second, but she convinced me to pursue my only real talent, which is art. I'm happy, have been clean (both cancer and pills) for 7 years now, and I own my own business.

At my age, I had to face it that no matter how good I could paint, I'd never make money at it till I was dead. So I "sold out" and went the graphic design route.

Moved to the Quad Cities with Steph and my son from previous marriage and our son from my now marriage (he's 5 now... at 46 years old, that's a trip in itself man) and got jobs at a few promotions companies till I built up a reputation kinda as THE designer in the area, especially when it came to Screen Print designs. After a couple years I quit my jobs and start my own company...

What are you doing now?

Upon visiting Asheville for a week we went back to Iowa, and sold everything, liquidated my business and moved to Asheville. Been here three months now and in two weeks my new shop opens in downtown Asheville. Called "Karma by Design," I'll be doing custom work on the spot with the ability to print instantly on my new state of the art direct-to-garment printer.

www.fkncreative.com
www.thatshirtsite.com
www.itskarmabydesign.com
Email: mark@fkncreative.com

Greg C.
Pure Aggression

1991 was a decidedly bleak year for me. I hit a wall in life regarding work, school and life in general. I needed to escape the corn fields of Northern IL. So I did.

I joined the USAF in September with a report date of March 15th, 1992. Little did I know that life was about to get interesting again just as I was ready to leave. My luck.

An old friend of mine made the trip from Rockford to DeKalb to track me down. It was Mark Snodgrass. He told me he had a nighttime radio show on WLUV and the Rockford hard rock / metal scene was going pretty strong. I hadn't been to a good local show in a long time.

He told me about bands like Decadenza, Stone Mason, Blind Witness and one band he was really into, Pure Aggression. He said I'd dig this band and he was right.

The more I got involved in music again the more I began to question my decision to join the Air Force. Looking back, it was both a good and bad thing for me.

I left Northern Illinois at a time when music was thriving and the scene was strong and opportunity was everywhere.

Mark called me one night and said we should all hang out together, talk, see if there was chemistry and there was, we all hit off right away.

Greg was a cool guy from the get go. He had an energy unbound that burned its way through Pure Aggression's music as well as Greg's personal and professional life. Fiercely dedicated, equally motivated.

If I remember correctly, we ended the night late at "*Uncle Nicks*" gyro place downtown Rockford by the bridge. It was a local hang for just about everyone I knew.

And that was it, we were off to the races after that. Pure Aggression is another band that made an indelible impression upon me. Great band, great guys, fun music and their shows were amazing as well.

How did the band start out?

Greg C: *It was the mid to late 1980's. At the time I had a few friends in high school. I felt like an outcast since I was a metal head.*

I was made fun of and bullied for being Polish and being a metal head. I was called a devil worshiper and got into fights with people over that shit.

I didn't drink, never been high, and went to church more often than many of the others in my Catholic school. Needless to say I fucking hated damn near everyone.

The few people I got along with at that time were either Metal Heads, or friends I had in the Martial Arts school I trained at.

Back then there was no internet so we used telephone modems and computers to dial BBS's (bulletin board systems) to connect with people. I got into that and met other people who had similar interests, specifically with music.

I met Mark Atkinson (guitars), Jim Gade (drums and guitar) and several others who became good friends and roommates when we left our parents homes.

Myself, Mark and Jim didn't meet face to face for a while but constantly typed with one another on the BBS about music and other stuff. If I remember correctly, one of the first times I ever met them was probably at a Zyklon B *(Later known as* Sarkoma*) show.*

The first local show I ever went to was Zyklon B *and* Bludgeoned Nun *(I think), New Year's Eve 1987-88 (?) in Loves Park. After that was T*he Accused, The Brotherhood, and Bludgeoned Nun *in downtown Rockford at Endless Nights.*

I tried to start a band in high school with the 2 close friends I had, but they were taking to long for me while they were working on their "musical style." I wanted it NOW.

The feeling I had going to a live metal / punk / hardcore show, being in the pit and getting out all my

38

frustration and aggression, was like no other feeling I ever had.

Metal was therapy for me, and shows were the ultimate way of connecting with myself and others, purely sharing in the love of music.

Once I had that live Metal / Punk / Hardcore show taste I wanted to be in a band and write music and lyrics. So I got closer to Mark and Jim and eventually we started jamming together. But we needed a base player.

Mark jammed with several others leading up to our sessions and one person that stood out to him was Jason Stewart.

We made a couple of crappy recordings on a boombox and Jason liked it and came over to check us out and saw something there. That was the beginning...

What were the initial expectations for Pure Aggression? Gig around as a local band, have fun or were there expectations that this would turn into a career?

It started out as some young kids that hated a lot of the world, loved Metal and just wanted to create something special to ourselves and share it with other pissed off youths.

Were there local bands that maybe inspired you to start a band or was it just the heavy hitters at the time like Cannibal Corpse, Deicide, etc.

We went to see Sarkoma, Bludgeoned Nun, forchristsake / Mirrored Image. *They were the big bands in the Rockford scene at that time. And one of my favorite "local" bands from Springfield, IL...NIL8.*
But there were many other bands brewing in Rockford -- Decadenza (later Watership Down), Atonement, Necrosis, Blind Witness, Devoid, *hell I can't remember all of them.*
ALL of us eventually played shows with each other and had a blast.
I became close with the guys in Sarkoma and Bludgeoned Nun. *I looked up to them musically and we had a mutual respect for one another. The music brought us together.*
*I spent a lot of time with Brian Carter (*Sarkoma*) going to the shooting range, camping, and training in martial arts (as well as the singer for BN, Ray Hart).*
*Even played softball on a team (we sucked but had fun!) with Tony (*Sarkoma/BN*) and Ray. I always got along with Stu and Mike "Hilly" as well. All those friendships are still strong today.*

Describe Rockford's metal / thrash scene back in the late 80's.

I got into the scene before I could drive and had to hitch rides with older kids or friend's parents to go to shows.
But as the 90's came in many of us were out of high school, had cars, and got out.
Bands came together, lots of practice, and then we scrounged money to get studio time in the back room of the music store "Jus Jammin" in Loves Park, where I got my first guitar.

Jimmy Johnson created "The Noise Chamber" recording Studio in the closet of the back room of that place. Most of us recorded our first cassettes there on reel to reel tape.

A big plug that helped the scene back then was Mark Snodgrass who started a local radio show called "Listen to This."

He began playing Sarkoma *and when we heard it we had to get our band on it! I remember talking to the guys in PA after a practice night at my parents' house while listening to the show.*

I said let's go find that station and give them our cassette. That was our first recording. Our first demo "A New Meaning of Death." I didn't know Mark at the time but dammit I wanted to get PA's music on the radio. We went down there, knocked on the door and gave Mark a tape.

Mark and I talked later on and we found that we both had a passion for local underground music and wanted to promote all of it and help the scene.

His radio show promoted our first show at the Cherry Lounge in February 91-92? We sold a ton of our cassettes and Mark said he never had his phones blow up for requests like that.

We were excited and couldn't wait to play our first show. As a matter of fact, I think that is the first night we met, Theron.

Then you gave me the opportunity to write for "Louder than God" and I had a blast interviewing and seeing my musical heroes play live. Because of that I went to so many shows and engulfed my life in music.

*Meeting everyone from Dave Mustaine (*Megadeth*) to Glen Danzig,* Vinny and Roger from Agnostic Front, DRI, *to being on the tour busses of* Cannibal Corpse *and* Obituary. *The list goes on...some of the best times of my life. Thanks man...*

Looking back on that scene, do you think Northern IL had a shot at becoming maybe the next "Sunset Strip" in terms of metal? What do you think would've taken it to the next level?

I think that we had a lot of talented bands but it was so hard to get support on places to play and advertising (after Mark got kicked off the air).
If we would have had more support on a higher level, maybe..." Sunset Strip" LOL -- never. Maybe in our own minds.

You did a demo that I believe was called "Trust No One." What were the expectations surrounding it, were you expecting to sell copies and maybe attract label interest?

It was actually called "A New Meaning of Death." "Trust No One" was written by me and another song that was played a lot on the radio was "Human Flesh" written by Mark, about Dahmer.
We just tried to get our music out, pay for our recording and hope we made more so we could save for better equipment and more studio time. We did hope to get some label interest too.

Was there any indie label interest in the band?

If I remember correctly, we may have sent our next recording "Hate" to Metal Blade *and* Columbia.

We did get some interest from Chaos Records, *a subsidiary of* Columbia. *I think Mark helped us with that one. I know he helped us make some videos to send to the labels as well.*

At that time Mark was a big part of helping us with art work, promotions and management. He had a talent and passion for the scene like no one else.

Did Pure Aggression ever get a chance to open up for any big name bands back then?

A good friend of ours who was also the singer for Necrosis, *John Cabrera began to get into promotions. He booked us a show with* Six Feet Under.

Was there ever any doubt in your mind about *not* going to college and doing PA full time and just trying to make it as a musician?

I have always been interested in bettering myself, be it through formal education, real world experience, reading, training in martial arts or training in firearms.

When I left high school I went to Rock Valley (community college), studied engineering with the possibility of taking over my parent's machine shop.

But when I started taking the math courses, I realized I sucked at math and I didn't have the passion for running a business.

I know I could make much more money and have better job security than music, but I wanted to do what I was passionate about.

"Cops" was on TV, I was always interested in possibly joining the military and I was always fascinated with good guys vs. bad guys.

I was reading "Solider of Fortune" magazines since I was in grade school, and day dreamed about helping the innocent and weak. So when a friend suggested I take a police science class it was a natural progression.

I learned more about all aspects of law enforcement agencies at the local, state, and federal level as well as our intelligence agencies. I began to read more about that as well as foreign affairs and international relations.

I was working part time, going to college, playing in PA, helping you with LTG (Louder Than God mag), *helping Mark Snodgrass with his TV show "Look At This", and going to the Kamishin Ryu Club (martial arts) ...I was constantly on the move man. I could not stop.*

However, once I got my Associate Degree in Police Science, I put more effort into the band to try and get us to the point of playing for a living. Yet, I still took a few classes on the side.

I did internships with the Rockford Police Department, and the Winnebago County Coroner's Office, all while working and promoting the band.

However, once the band was near the end, I always said I would leave town, get a Bachelor's Degree in

Administration of Justice, and work as a Federal Agent in a Law Enforcement Agency.

My whole life I wanted to be a warrior. That was my strongest passion, helping others and fighting for what is right. While going to school I spent my money on going to shooting schools and getting trained up.

Others blew money on drugs and booze, I spent mine on outdoor equipment, guns, gear, and training.

I ended up meeting my wife during that time, finished a Master's Degree and I currently work for the Federal Government in Law Enforcement as a Special Agent.

I feel like I am the luckiest man alive. I have my dream job, wife, and kids. Now my passion is to spend time with my wife, son and daughter.

Eventually when I get closer to retirement I may work towards a PhD, and teach at a university, while training others in firearms at a tactical shooting school.

In my travels in life, especially being involved in the underground music scene, I have learned so much from a diverse group of people.

I have learned tolerance, forgiveness, and standing up and fighting for what is right. Even when we didn't see eye to eye on drinking, drugs, and politics, (which happened a lot for me). We respected each other and loved each other because of our passion for music.

All those things helped build my character and allowed me to love life more.

Pure Aggression didn't make it to the year 2000. When did you personally know the end was near for the band?

Working on our last recording in 96. Jim and Jason were gone a few years back, so the only original members were me and Mark.

The other guys who came in later gave us so much musically and we became close friends but they wanted to go into other directions. We were all fighting a lot over BS, stress, frustration, etc.

Jason West, who came to play drums for us had the opportunity to travel with a signed blues act and make some money.

Paul Macaluso was getting close with the guys in Watership Down *(formally* Decadenza*) and wanted to play with them. Micky Rosenquist was tired of it too.*

So when Jason left to go and tour, Paul and Micky were done also so I said fuck it, I'm out of this town, and going to school far away from here.

I will say though, Jason, Paul, and Micky created some of our BEST shit. It was a great team and great time.

I still love and respect all of those guys, I still feel lucky to have played with all the guys in P.A. I still believe that they are some of the most talented musicians and artists I know.

PURE AGGRESSION

Greg Czaczkowski
Jim Gade
Mark Atkinson
Jason Stewart

ARSENAL MANAGEMENT
MAC-10 MUSIC
P.O. Box
Rockford, Illinois
(815)

Do you have any regrets not taking Pure Aggression further?

I don't regret a damn thing I have done in life. Mistakes and all, they make me who I am.

I feel like I had the best of different worlds...music, law enforcement, and the best family life I could have ever imagined. Everything happens for a reason.

I love all the steps I have taken to get where I am now, and I am grateful for the highs and lows.

Any plans to re-release the band's demo or other music on iTunes in the future?

We did a 20-year reunion show a few years back and had a BLAST!

Jason West asked me about re-recording the songs before him as well as the ones we did together. Just talk at this point.

We are all busy with our lives, but I do hope we can make it happen in the near future.

47

Is there a Facebook page or website you'd like to plug?

Check out Pure Aggression *on Facebook. Mark Atkinson put our last recording which was done on CD, on Reverbnation. Also just YouTube Pure Aggression.*
That last show we did was professionally video recorded by Brock Hutzler and he put up some music videos of the show...I also posted some OLD PA stuff as well...check it out and enjoy!

What about your band members? Where they and what are they doing?

Mark Atkinson is a manager at his work where he has been for over 25 years. He's still playing music and teaching his young son the power of metal.
Jim Gade is married, and is using his artistic talents as a multi-media manager for the Rockford Ice Hogs, Metro Center, and Harris Bank Center.
Jason Stewart married with four kids and is a Deacon at my old Catholic church in Rockford and teaches religion at my old Catholic high school.
Paul Macaluso is married with kids and works in the cellular industry and still plays music.
Jason West is married, lives in Texas, and is a "hired gun" in music. He has toured the world with several different bands and styles of music and continues to do so. I can't list all the bands he has toured/recorded with.
Micky Rosenquist is married with two kids, teaches music at the Rock and Roll Institute, and is a singer, songwriter, and performer and runs Underground Squirrel Studio.
I recently moved back to Northern IL and I work in Chicago with the same agency after working for nearly 10 years in NYC. Don't play guitar or write songs anymore. Although I have introduced my kids to the guitar and metal.

I am a firearms instructor for my agency, still train outside of work (as well as at work), play with HAM (amateur radio) radio, backpack and camp.

My biggest hobby and guilty pleasure is Swiss watches. I collect a few, and hope to have more someday. And at this rate I will probably work in the watch industry.

Brian Carter
Sarkoma

Sarkoma was a band whose name kept popping up when you talked about the local scene.

It wasn't until I was doing my zine "*Louder Than God*" that I finally got around to interviewing the band at their debut gig after getting signed with Chicago based label "*Grindcore Records.*" And what a show it was.

The venue was a small bar outside of Belvidere gigging with forchristsake. To say it was a fun exciting time would be an understatement. Great show, oddball location. What year was Sarkoma started?

Brian Carter (Vocals): *1987 in Aaron Ingrams garage just the two of us. I was playing guitar at that point.*

How did the band members come together?

50

Stu and Mike came into the band around same time as Aaron and i. we then moved it to Mikes basement where it stayed till it's end.

Was your personal goal to take Sarkoma nationwide and be a working musician or keep the band local and maybe consider school?

At this point in my life all I wanted was to be a rock star, like Dave says " I lived my life like there was no tomorrow..."

Prior to be signed, was Sarkoma playing just Northern IL or all over the Midwest?

We did mostly midwest shows. Loved doing all aged shows kids appreciate music more than drunks in bars...

What larger name bands did Sarkoma do shows with?

We never really did too many shows with bigger bands that I can remember.

Do you remember that one point in time when it occurred to you that maybe Sarkoma could be bigger than just a local band, that maybe, just maybe you could score a record deal?

Of course that was when I heard us on the radio for the first time, but I never really thought much about what it was going to become. Just played rocked and let it live.

Who found who when it came to Grindcore Records?

A friend at the time was managing us (Nick Senave) he was working at Grindcore and asked me to give him a demo next thing we know we get signed on my 21st birthday.

At that point in time the Rockford metal scene was pretty active. Were you thinking that maybe Rockford could've been the next big metal scene outside of LA?

No never crossed my mind.

Looking back at that era, what's your opinion now, all these years later? Do you think Rockford could've been the next big metal scene?

Not really, Rockford has always had great talent but without other like minded clubs and bars or places for these talented people to play, it makes it pretty hard.

I believe you did two records with Grindcore -- "Integrity" and "Completely Different." Were you able to tour the country for both records, if so, what bands did you tour with?

The only tour we did had ¾ of the shows cancelled before we showed up, it was a great learning expierence. Made it all the way to mexico and back...good times.

What happened between Grindcore Records and Sarkoma? I believe the label went out of business, right?

Ya but our 2nd CD was on Redlight records same label different name and different bands, more commercial bands.

Was there any label interest in the band post Grindcore?

Ya Redlight.

What led to the dissolution of the band, what were the factors involved?

Two people wanted to go in different directions and they did. I wanted to get more heavy and one wanted to play rap rock, guess what one I am????

Was it a good split or bad split?

Bad.

Why not revisit Sarkoma now?

All members have moved on, and too much time has come between us.

Any plans to make Sarkoma music available on iTunes?

Not sure.

So let's work up to the video shoot and the record release party. Which came first or were they bundled together?

Yes, they were together, but the video never happened. The people that were going to shoot the video i.e. MTV or whoever never showed up or gave any reason as to why. Go figure...

Who chose the song for the video, the band or the record company?

We had full artistic control over all decisions in Sarkoma.

Who came up with idea to do the record release party? Was that the band or the label and how did the venue get chosen?

The idea for a record release party was the bands idea, and "reflections" was a place we all hung out at so it was an easy choice.

54

I'm curious, why not Rotation Station, were they closed then or not doing locals shows anymore?

Rotation station was awesome; great place. We shot our first video there with a few awesome skaters. Jim Feterly was going to college in Chicago and hooked us up with a film company named "kundalini films." It was never released to the public.

I am not sure why the ball was dropped on that one but it was a cool video. Not sure why or what happened to lead Rotation Station to stop doing shows. I'm sure it was because of a change in ownership.

![SARKOMA]

Who paid for the video shoot, the band or the label?

The label did not pay for anything LMAO....

Was the record release party a success? If I remember correctly, wasn't MTV supposed to have covered it for Headbangers Ball?

The record party was great, but as I said before there was no video shoot. The label failed on all aspects of their part of that.

Did Sarkoma ever play Metalfest in Milwaukee?

Yes, Sarkoma played METALFEST along with 30 other bands lol, those things are a train wreck.

Post Sarkoma 2014. What are you doing now? Do you know what the other band members are doing?

Well after I was in a way more successful band called The Heavils *we were signed to* Metal Blade Records *for 5 years. We put out 2 CD's and toured with some awesome bands.*

Got to open for Slipknot *3 times, opened for* Slayer, *toured with* Six Feet Under, the Red Chord, Misery signals, Bloodhound Gang.

Devin Townsend *produced our second release "Heavilution." We were in Guitar Player Magazine twice, Guitar world, Rolling Stone. This was my proudest achivement in music.*

Why not reform Sarkoma with other members and march on? Other bands have done it. Same thing with The Heavils. Why not just get other musicians and move on? Both bands were killer.

Sarkoma *would never reform, personal differences.* The Heavils *haven't died. Myself and the former drummer Toast are working on a project as we speak. We will be recording soon and will be playing shows as well.*

The Heavils

56

Brian Carter

The Heavils

Glenn Rene Zeringue Junior
Bludgeoned Nun

If you would, please introduce yourself, what instrument you played in the band and a brief bio of Bludgeoned Nun as well.

What years was Bludgeoned Nun active?'

85-'90-ish

Did the band release any demos or records during that time?

We did have a bunch of garage recordings. A lot from live shows.

I noticed there's no BN on iTunes. Any plans to release any music on there?

All of the archived stuff I had (recordings, fliers etc) were wiped out during hurricane Katrina. There is a complete live show on SoundCloud.

Was Bludgeoned Nun meant to be a fun party type band or did you guys have aspirations of trying to take the band national, maybe snag a record deal?

No record deal. The whole point was to do it ourselves

Was there any record label interest in the band?

None

Was the Rockford punk / hardcore scene known outside of Rockford? Was it ever mentioned in other zines around the country or maybe in Maximum Rock N Roll?

Yes, it was known. I don't really know about media wise but it was known to people in the scene

Bands like Operation Ivy, Verbal Abuse and I think SNFU all came through Rockford at some point doing basement shows and such.

How did those shows get set up and can you relate some of those experiences for us? Were the bands cool, did they stay overnight at someone's house?

Bands were booked through word of mouth or grapevine. The hardest part was finding venues. I was involved with getting the Descendants *there (they stayed at my house).*

*Usually someone who knew someone who knew someone with a space would say. "Let's do a show" and it would go from there. We played a party in an abandoned building at one point so the "*happening*" was where you made it*

When Black Flag played Rockford it seemed like that energized not just the punk / hardcore scene but the Rockford music scene in general. Was that show really that much of a landmark in Rockford's music history?

Oh yeah but Rockford's "scene" was really just a part of Chicago / Madison etc. And you just drove to the venue. It didn't really matter where it was.

How much did the local punk / hardcore scene really reap from Black Flag playing Rockford, were there more people at the shows, more merch sold, etc?

Dunno man. People really just "did" instead of analyzing what - where impact. I had a blast so that's a good thing

How those did gigs get set up and was venue management supportive or cautious of the punk / metal gigs that took place there?

Venues were the hardest to obtain. We played in a corn field at one point. Wagon Wheel, Rockton IL? Or something like that.

Being we had no money places like VFW halls and wedding reception halls were out. We just made do. Basements...lots & lots O' basements

Was Rockford's punk / hardcore scene active and dynamic back then or was it closed off and not well supported?

It was pretty active. A lot of bands came through. What sucked was trying to get support from everyone.
The Dead Milkmen played for us, literally US, all 5 of us. Sad. The Midwest outside of Chicago or Minneapolis really doesn't have live music culture. It definitely isn't NOLA.

[Flyer: OPERATION IVY from Berkely California / BLUDGEONED NUN from Rockford Illinios / Monday April 11th / Show starts 6:30 PM / 3 dollars / 3909 11th street, Howard Johnson's Hotel, past the bypass]

Looking back on it now do you still feel the same way?

Yes

Why did the band break up?

You know I really don't know. I really wanted to study "music" and not being from there I wanted to go see something else

Musically speaking, what has life post Bludgeoned Nun been like for you, what have you been up to? Post fleeing Rockford?

Large subject. Master's degree in Music from University of New Orleans. I did my undergrad at Berklee college of Music, Boston. Performance major.
Today I'm really just into honest music, that's why I like Jazz because it's immediate and live in your face.
I still do corporate band gigs. Have no problem butchering the latest "junktry" tune for your father\daughter dance. PAY ME!
The style\genre doesn't really matter as long as it's honest. I still maintain a solo portfolio of orchestral pieces even though I don't get to play 'em that often.

Are you still in Rockford? If not, why did you leave?

Not in Rockford no mo'. I'm kinda a wandering Jew. Don't really stay too long anywhere. Big world, lots to see kinda thing.

Are you still active in the punk or hardcore scene where you are? Still listen to punk / hardcore?

Still into bands and music now but with symphonic and educated music thrown in.

Looking back now, do you think Bludgeoned Nun was instrumental in helping to launch or maybe progress the Rockford punk / hardcore scene back then?

I don't really know man. Y'all would know better. I haven't been there in 20+ years. Would love to do a reunion show!

64

Dan Gildea
PineWood Box

What brought all the band members together to create PineWood Box? Did you all have a mutual desire to make punk music together?

Dan Gildea: *I believe Paul and the other members wanted to play music for fun, but also desired to play professionally; making enough money to support themselves without having to work other jobs. I got involved in* PineWood Box *and the Rockford music scene coming from a different direction altogether. In my case, I never expected to ever be in a band. I wasn't a musician. I went to school for visual art.*
   Paul didn't recruit me to be in his band right away. I became acquainted with Paul Kissick after seeing him in bars

and at parties. It was a while before I even knew he had been in bands like Near Mrs. and Juicy Fiancé. After Paul got to know me he discovered I was an artist and sculptor and I had done a lot of work for local haunted house attractions. (Dark Attractions).

He asked me to help him with a band he wanted to put together that would have great stage shows. He used The Damned as an example. He invited me to sit in on practices they were having at Nick Thomas' house on Lapey Street. Between sessions we would sit around and talk about shows we'd seen, ideas we had for stage shows, etc. My challenge was to build props and sets for their shows with a $0 budget.

After a while we all became friends. Eventually, one evening, Paul pulled over an old broken living room organ and asked me to play it. I told him I couldn't play it because I wasn't a musician. He said "Neither are we." and insisted I press the keys. Nick would help me by figuring out the notes on his bass and show me what keys I needed to press. I learned the root notes of all the early PineWood Box songs this way.

After a while I'd advance my own method of making chords using three stiff fingers in a sort of Wolverine-like hand position. Much later, Nathan Kaddutz would show me how the actual chords were meant to be played. (I'd played them wrong for so long, the actual chords sounded weird!)

What was the goal of the band? Stay local, keep it loose, or be serious, release records, tour, snag a record deal?

After a while I think, at the very least, we all had aspirations of playing out enough to live on the income of the band. I think the thought of a tour was also imagined.

Can you describe the punk scene in Rockford back in the 80's? Was it well organized, active dynamic or just the opposite?

There was a lot of music going on in Rockford in the 80's. A number of bands identified as "punk." There was no real representation for the bands. The bands themselves would submit tapes to bars and events who would pick and choose from the musical buffet as the wished. I think why we did well in the environment was because we generally promised a visual show or production of some sort.

How receptive was Rockford (venue owners, etc.) to punk rock back then? Were people hassled by the police, were there problems getting venues booked, etc.?

I would say generally pretty receptive. There were no "clubs" that catered to any particular kind of music, just bars who seemed willing to let most anyone play from what I could tell. We even played country bars and were well received by the audience.

I don't remember any problems with the police other than what you might expect with any drunken or disorderly behavior. Certainly no problems generated by bands identifying or playing punk music; i.e., vulgarity, profanity or vandalism. All the bands I remember lasting were pretty professional.

Was there a network between bands in say, Rockford, Madison and Milwaukee, where Madison bands played Rockford, Rockford bands play Milwaukee, etc? Was it that well organized?

There was some crossover. We played a number of out of town shows and when bands from out of town played here we were often hired as the opener. I can't say it was organized, however. There was no management or organization that promoted or facilitated the schedules and transportation of the bands at the level we were working.

A lot of bigger name punk bands made their way through Rockford back then -- Alice Donut, Dead Milkmen, Black Flag, Fugazi, etc. Do you remember who was promoting these shows and how well attended they were?

I remember a number of those shows. I don't know if they were self-managed by the bands or by management companies. They were working at a level above us.

Do you think getting those bands into Rockford for gigs drew more attention to the local bands, scene, etc?

Probably. We and other local band would open for the traveling headliners. Big shows that were played well would generate a lot of t-shirt and cassette sales for us.

Rockford had a diverse cross section of local bands playing back then. Did the various scenes intermingle with each other, that is, did the metal scene crossover into punk and vice versa, did bands of different genres hang out together, attend each other's shows or were battle lines drawn?

There was definitely a lot of camaraderie among bands of various genres. I can't think of any conflict that was generated out of musical genre differences.

What about Rockford's music scene now, as good or not as good as it was back in the 80's and 90's?

The 80's and 90's seemed like a good time for all kinds of music. I can't say that the music genres are as diverse as they used to be, but I know musicians and technicians are making music every weekend here in Rockford.

Looking back on the scene now, was it as strong as you remember? Why or why not?

Well, PineWood Box was together for 11 years. 8 of those years my only income came from doing shows, my expenses were low back then, but still, I didn't starve and I had a roof over my head, so it was good enough, I played enough shows each week, to support me for 8 years. I think that's pretty good.

Why did PineWood Box eventually split up?

After a while, as we got older and gained more responsibilities in our lives, it got harder and harder to make ends meet with just the income from playing out. We eventually had to get real jobs. (Real jobs is the part of life that will hollow you out faster than anything.) It became harder and harder to schedule practice and arrange shows.

After Nick's death and numerous member changes, it got to the point where we'd only be doing several special shows a month. After a while, even that slowed.

Paul was working in other bands, most notably The Savants, making great music, but much simpler shows. It was always a possibility that Paul and I would work on PineWood Box projects, again, but then he was murdered back in 2000. That drove the last nail, so to speak, in PineWood Box ever performing again.

So present day, what are you currently up to?

Musically, I have worked on some Internet music projects and I have guest appeared with a couple bands over the years, but I never played out as a member of another band. I work with computers and teachers at Kinnikinnick School District in Roscoe IL. I still work on public art projects with a crew of artists and technicians, usually under the name ScaryHouse.com.

I know PineWood Box has a new record on iTunes called "Embalmed." Is the band back together again?

"Embalmed" is a collection of all the cassette demo tapes we made plus several live tracks from shows, remastered and preserved on the Internet.

We recorded three demo tapes:

PineWood Box - Opens Up (1985)
PineWood Box - Shadows (1988)
PineWood Box - The Poor, The Unknown (1991)

Dave Ensminger
PineWood Box

I was trying to remember where and when it was I met Dave Ensminger. It wasn't at a music gig but most likely at a poetry reading he and my father took part in back in the 80's, downtown Rockford,

I recall going to Appletree Records with my dad shortly before I left Illinois in the spring of '92. Really miss that place. That and Toad Hall.

They had a staggering collection of underground / import punk and metal that kept me coming back dropping hundreds of bucks on tapes, records, zines and concert t-shirts. I never left Appletree without buying something. That was blasphemy.

Appletree was a mecca for music fans and bands alike. Black Flag and Gone did an autograph signing there before their infamous Rockford gig June 16th, 1986 at The Channel. Local bands flyer'd the hell out of this joint.

This time felt different. This visit had a feeling of finality to it. I was leaving the area and knew I wasn't coming back, at least not any time soon. As much as I didn't want to leave home I needed distance and time to get my act together.

Dave was working there at the time my father and I came in so he and my dad struck up a conversation while I got lost in the grandeur of Appletree.

I walked out with a Killdozer tape, a Venom CD ("Black Metal") and a Celtic Frost t-shirt. I think I spoke to Dave briefly, via my father, and then we left. Dave, himself, would leave about a year later.

I knew of him as a poet back in the day but not as the punk historian he's become now. Musician, author, folklorist. Ensminger has seen and done it which made him the perfect person to contact when I decided to undertake this project. His grasp of punk history then and now is astounding to say the least.

You were certainly an integral part of the Rockford punk scene back in the 80's. Can you give us a quick rundown of how you were involved?

To be fair, I always thought I was the kid who was close to the kids that were more integral – that is, in terms of my age group: the teenagers of the mid-1980s.

My sister knew the older subset, like Dan from Pinewood Box, since both attended Harlem High School together.

I had a pick-up band with her friends that would play shows at house parties, so I learned to play tunes like "Nervous Breakdown" by Black Flag *when I was around thirteen.*

I was linked to the folks at Rotation Station because I went to school with Rory, whose mother owned the place, and I both played and attended shows all the time there (from Capitol Punishment *and* The Adolescents *to* Swiz *and* Verbal Assault *and* Life Sentence*).*

Then I linked up with teens like Tad Keyes, Chris Furney, and Jeremy Kunz, partially because my fanzine "No Deposit No Return" was in full force.

Plus, I was one of the few drummers that could play a blend of vintage punk, frenetic hardcore, and fluid emo, so I could play with metal heads, straight-edge kids, and older guys who were into what later became the sound of Touch and Go Records, Amphetamine Reptile, *and the like.*

Later, I ended up working at Appletree Records *with people from Beloit College, so I quickly latched on to that scene as well.*

Do you remember what year you got into punk rock, just listening to it? Who were the bands you were into?

74

I always give credit to my brother and sister. Starting in winter 1980/81, Michael would bring home a variety of LPs, 7"s, and fanzines that completely re-shaped my world.

The first three I recall vividly were Siouxsie and the Banshees, PIL, *and* Cockney Rejects, *but quickly he would give me everything from* Joy Division *to* Butthole Surfers.

In the meantime, my sister was a devotee of Iggy Pop, David Bowie, Lene Lovich, Psychedelic Furs, Gun Club, *but also blues like* Howlin' Wolf.

So, I was warped from the beginning, it seems. One day my world was Cheap Trick, The Kings, and Buggles, *but by fifth grade I was writing reports about* Johnny Rotten / Lydon*!*

What was your first punk show and where was it? Were you hooked after that?

My sister's boyfriend took me to see local power pop unit The Flex *in DeKalb at some joint near the university, where one could smoke opium and not even blink or worry.*

75

We listened to X's *second record, on tape, there and back. My next gig was* Black Flag, *and my hearing loss suffered next to that P.A. still affects me!*

How would you characterize Rockford's punk scene back in the 80's looking back on it now?

Was it as good or bad as you remember it? What stands out in your mind?

For a while, I rarely went to gigs in Madison or Chicago because so many shows occurred within the Rockford area.

In fact, I became rather choosy, opting not to see Scream *(too long haired, too rock) or* Uniform Choice *(too long haired, too rock) by the late 1980s.*

In some ways I regret those decisions, but I was a fairly doctrinaire punk and felt they betrayed their earlier roots.

Punk rock has always been very personal to me, an extension of one's ethos, value systems, worldviews, etc., so I lived a code.

The other thing I regret: not taking nearly enough photos, which leaves great gaps in my memories.

Paul Kissick, Dan Gildea and Nick Thomas.

Now, I shoot most of the pics for my own articles and books, to retain the DIY sense, but also because I don't want moments to blur, gray out, overlap, or diffuse.

If we're documenting punk history in Rockford, what bands do we need to mention / talk about?

Record stores, from Appletree Records *to* Toad Hall *to* Denzil's Record Emporium *in Beloit and more.*

They were epicenters – for local DIY product, conversations galore, a variety of promotional music items that are now lost to history, some gigs (like Gone!*), to rubbing elbows with people like* Cheap Trick.

What about local zines and record labels?

I have PDFs of all my zines, if you want them too. Other Rockford zines were few are far between. I know kids made them: I just don't have any copies, minus some lit journals.

Do you remember Rockford's scene being cohesive or was it kind of scattered?

Well, the scene was cohesive to a degree due to the paucity of clubs. For a while, most shows happened at Rotation Station *and* Dartbee's, *or bars like* Endless Nights, Tinkers Lounge, *and the basement of* Cherry Lounge, *or places like* Polish Falcons Club *and VFW halls. So, yes, some of those places are a half hour apart.*
There was no central district or strip like I experienced in Albuquerque. Plus, the all-ages kids like me had to fend for ourselves: build ramps and stages, rent equipment, and run Xerox flyers, maybe host a radio show in Beloit, like I did, starting in the summer of 1989. But we all felt more or less in the same ship.
The older guys eventually accepted us as well, as we aged and joined more "mature" bands, like Becky's Birthday, *who opened for* Fugazi.
They sounded like a cross between late-period Die Kreuzen *and* The Cult. *Then, of course, were bands like* War on the Saints, *who were like prog punk, really adept musicians. They sounded in the late-1990s Dischord vein*

*(*Scream, Kingface*), where* Bludgeoned Nun *could really play too but were almost precursors to grindcore and screamo.*

We had Fugazi, Verbal Abuse, Operation Ivy, etc. performing shows in Rockford but it's the Black Flag show that everyone remembers and talks about.
    Why is that and do you think that show in particular helped move the scene forward, bring more attention to it?

Not really. All kinds of gigs pre-dated that, like Eugene Chadbourne, The Replacements, Naked Raygun, *and more, but that show did earn press coverage.*

I think I still have the clipping from the Rockford Register Star, and it also witnessed an outsized police presence.

I remember the cops lining the streets afterwards, telling me, "Get your ass home boy," or something just like that.

Ironically, the riot days of Black Flag *were well behind them: in fact, they were like a mock-rock band that barely played any of their old material, minus a half-winking, sartorial version of* "Gimme Gimme Gimme."

For me, the next important shows were The Adolescents, *because I made my first flyer for it, and* Capitol Punishment *because I played their drum kit, received sincere, generous feedback, and knew that I was never gonna shed my punk skin.*

But that's just a few – incredible SNFU *shows,* Youth of Today *shows,* Swiz *shows, all happened. And more.*

What bands were you involved in back in the 80's in Rockford's punk scene?

I cut a three-song demo with my straight-edge band Vital Signs, *maybe in the 9th grade, and we even lacked a bass player, but it didn't stop us, though the Christian studio made us censor the word shit.*

Then I drummed with Honeycomb Hideout, *who opened for* Kingface *(Dischord Records), which later morphed into* Insight, *who opened for* 7 Seconds *in Madison and cut a demo reviewed in "Maximum RocknRoll."*

Later, I joined Geraldo, *then* Toe, *in Beloit. Flyers and photos for all those bands can be seen on my Midwest punk blog.*

79

You wound up writing for a lot of heavy duty mags, Maximum Rock N Roll being one of them.

What article did you do for them and how did you get it published, was it an open submission to them? What year was that?

I did not actually publish for MRR until the mid-2000s, when I submitted an article about Biscuit of the Big Boys.

Before he died, I drummed for him and edited his work in my magazine for about five years.

From there, I started publishing interviews with bands like Articles of Faith, *the* Fix, Beefeater, *and more, and to this day I still contribute.*

This Fall, my interviews with Frightwig *and* Raw Power *were published.*

Did you ever do any scene reports or articles about Rockford's punk scene in any zines / mags you wrote for?

Of course. You can see portions discussed in my book Visual Vitriol, *and my blog on "Midwestern Punk" documents literally everything I own that relates back to the scene.*

Are you still doing "Left of the Dial?" What's it about and where can we find it?

Nope, that is the past. It ran from 2000-2005 and is a collector's item.

Portions were re-published in my books Left of the Dial *and* Mavericks *as well as my App, found on iTunes --* Punk and Indie Rock Compendium: Left of the Dial.

80

So, I have tried to make the material as accessible as possible.

You've got several great books about punk rock published, can you talk about them and where do we find them?

Everywhere! <u>Left of the Dial</u> *and* <u>Mavericks</u> *contains interviews with the "icons" of the roots rock, punk rock, and indie rock movements and collect portions of my massive interview archive (well over 1,000 pages).*

<u>Visual Vitriol</u> *is a scholarly, folklore examination of the street art and cultures of the punk and hardcore generations, with a special look at graffiti and stenciling, skate culture, gays and lesbians, Hispanics and African Americans, and women too.*

What year did you leave Rockford and why?

I left with my first wife in 1993 to live in New Mexico to be close to my poetry mentor at the time, your father Todd Moore.

I attended the creative writing program at the College of Santa Fe. I have not lived in the Midwest since...

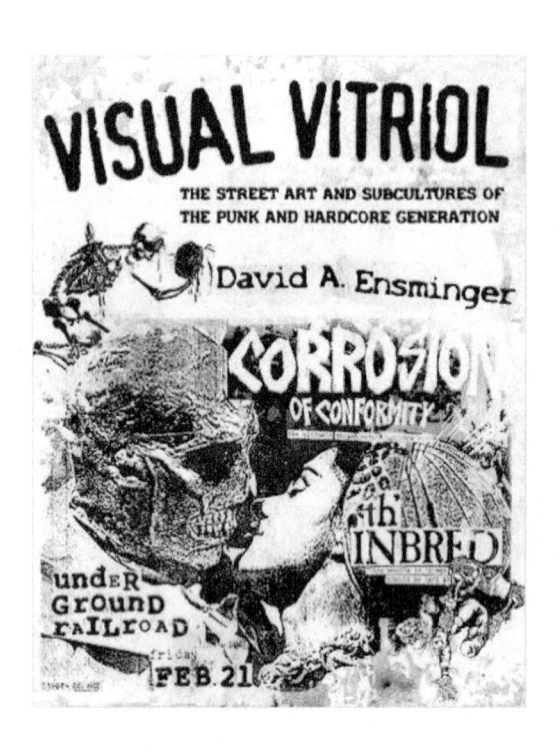

What's your current situation today, where are you and what are you up to?

I am a punk scholar and folklorist, an educator, a writer, a drummer, a book publisher and editor, an archivist, a husband, and photographer. Well, at least that's part of what I do!

A Short History of Punk and Indie Rock in Rockford, Illinois
By Dave Ensminger

Beyond Cheap Trick / A Quick Look at Illinois' True Second City (1980s – 1990s): Rockford, IL

Usually considered a restful hub during the boring trek between Chicago and Madison, Wisconsin, the mid-sized town of Rockford, Illinois, a former rust belt factory fiefdom, was home to premier power pop band Cheap Trick, 1980's porn star Ginger Lynn, Brad Wood (producer and engineer for Seam, Liz Phair, Veruca Salt, and many more) and future members of Die Kreuzen (Touch and Go), Tar (Touch and Go), and EIEIO (Frontier Records).

Though it does not share the punk legacy of the university towns of its Wisconsin neighbor or the feisty art and hardcore scenes of mammoth and mythic urban Windy City, it does have its own share of interesting stories. For instance, in the shadow of Cheap Trick were the overlooked "one-hit" efforts of The Names, who released the terrific single "Why Can't It Be," eventually featured on the Rhino compilation "Come Out and Play – American Power Pop (1975-78)."

Notable garage rock bands from the early 1980s include Davey and The Daggerz, (who were like the Gun Club), the tough'n'tumble rockabilly act Rocky and the Squirrels, and The Sharp Turn, who had a track on the notorious Battle of the Garages Vol. II (Voxx Records, 1984). In fact, slightly abrasive popsters the Vertebrats, from nearby Champaign, IL, contributed a track to the first volume (1981).

Meanwhile, around 1980, a few post-punk refugees from Rockford escaped to Milwaukee to form Tense Experts, a favorite band of Keith (bassist) from Die Kreuzen, who have a track, described as "dark, compelling postcards from the edge of oblivion" on the History in Three Chords CD compilation. Note: Keith (bass) and Dan (singer) from Die

Kreuzen starting playing music in Rockford with their band The Stellas.

Power pop bands in the mid-1980s included The Flex, who released the record "From the Vacuum" in 1985 (on which Brad Wood plays saxophone and saw blade), while harder neo-punk (think the Clash) bands from the era include The Icks, who put a record out on the label Fever, and Pinewood Box, a longtime band that mixed somewhat traditional 1970's-punk with a knack for keyboard experimentation (Suicide, late Wire…), but it was after Black Flag played downtown on its last tour that the scene really kicked into high gear, especially after Wisconsinite Tad Keyes moved in, and along with a handful of people, set up shows at various rented halls (VFW, Polish Falcons Club, basement shows etc) that included assorted hard-working touring bands of the era, including SNFU, NOFX, Dag Nasty, Operation Ivy, Fugazi, etc.

At the same time, and even before, a roller skating rink (Rotation Station) on the outskirts of town began hosting skateboard nights and touring bands too, culminating in powerful performances by Capital Punishment, Psycho, Flag of Democracy, the Adolescents, Swiz, and many more. In addition, the skate rock emporium was able to support regional heavies like Life Sentence, the Defoliants (future No Empathy), and more metallish Generation Waste. This was where many local bands found a strong following, the most notorious being the gritty, fierce, and ferocious Bludgeoned Nun, who later released a compilation on CD after their salad days.

Other strong bands included We Hate Cake, who eventually reformed as the more progressive punk styled War on the Saints. Surprisingly, they released a self-titled extended EP on Positive Force (7 Seconds) records in Jan. 1987. At the time, the line-up included Vince Jumapao, Bill Dolan, Scott Thompson and Kevin Hutchins. Later, they released a German CD titled "Who Ya Makin' Happy" with a new line-up whose sound resembled Kingface.

More significantly, guitarist Bill Dolan, known for his prowess, later moved to Chicago, forming 5ive Style with drummer John Herndon of Tortoise, and released two records on Sub Pop. He also played guest guitar on the demo by Insight, local Rockford emo style punk, which was reviewed by Maximum Rock'n' Roll in 1988.

Insight's guitarist, Jeremy Kunz, also a show promoter, later played guitar for Dryhouse and Beggars, an indie rock band in the vein of Ride, who were signed in the 1990s to Island records and released a 1995 record, with video ("Lovely Soul Detonator"). Insight featured No Deposit/No Return zine editor David Ensminger on drums, who later founded Left of the Dial magazine and web site.

Other key figures included Weasel Walters, whose love of confrontation and a mix of heady art rock PIL and free jazz pioneer Albert Ayler led him to form Chernobyl Children and other short lived bands. However, he too immigrated to Chicago and became a formidable presence in the 1990s, and even today, forming the much-lauded noise-jazz-punk outfit The Flying Luttenbachers.

In terms of heavy, instrumental riffage, the obscure but powerful Here were around, including former Mecht Mensch (early 1980s Madison hardcore band) bass player and noted skateboarder Brad Burnell, drummer Stu Patterson (formerly of The Sharp Turn), and sound engineer Scott Colborn, who has worked frequently with Sun City Girls and a large list of other projects.

Burnell also played on the 7" single by Rod Myers & The Ramps ("Wheelchair"/"Maybelline"), dubbed "dis-abilly" because Rod was a disabled rocker (and featured on the primetime show "Real People"), which was released on Subterranean Records (Code of Honor).

From the goth scene came The Wake RSV, inspired by the Sisters of Mercy, who reached large audiences in Chicago, while on the metalcore/crossover side, 1980's Harlem High School rockers Sarkoma, who absorbed a love for Fishbone and Celtic Frost, eventually toured and released two CDs in the 1990s, "Integrity" and "Completely Different," on Red Light and Grindcore Records.

-David Ensminger/Stu Patterson

https://midwestpunk.wordpress.com/2011/04/15/a-short-history-of-punk-and-indie-rock-in-rockford-il/

```
The PIT: 3210 Williams Ave. / Rockford, IL / 1996
------------------------------------------------------------
--------------------
Jan 13 Sat    *Quincy Punx / Apostles Of Gein / 1096 /
The Reacharounds // 7:00 $5
Jan 20 Sat    *Alligator Gun / Chanticleer / The Mashers
/ Figurehead // 7:00 $5
Feb 01 Thu    *Buck-o-Nine / The Eclectics / General
River / Yore // 7:00 $5
Feb 09 Fri    *Bollweevils / Mushuganas / Apocalypse
Hoboken / Eighteen // 7:00 $5
Feb 10 Sat Slapstick / Mulligan Stew / Slurr // 7:00 $5
Feb 25 Sun    *Mr. T Experience / The Smugglers / Boris
The Sprinkler // 7:00 $5
Mar 17 Sun    *Skankin' Pickle // 7:00 $6 /(unconfirmed)
Mar 27 Wed    *Let's Go Bowling // 7:00 $6/(unconfirmed)
```

Jerry Sofran
forchristsake

There were many local bands in the 80's hard rock / metal scene in Rockford I dug but forchristsake was at the top of my list.

I loved their music, their live shows plus they were just the coolest, most down to Earth guys to hang out with.

I was invited to their 4th Street apartment several times and it was always a great time. 25 years later those memories are still strong with me.

Of all the bands I knew, Sarkoma and forchristsake should've been the breakouts, should've had national success stories but for reasons I don't understand that success eluded them.

Before being called forchristsake the band was known as Mirrored Image. Tell me about the origin of the band and how all of you came to know each other.

Also, do you remember what the musical influences were that guided Mirrored Image musically?

Mirrored Image had been playing the Rockford music scene in the late 80's before I joined. I was playing in Rude Awakening with Jason Williams, and when he joined Mossy and Mirrored Image, *he brought me with in '89. Musically at that time thrash ruled, and you can hear our take on it with such songs as "Horace" and "On Your Grave."*

Oh man – we listened to and were influenced by it all back then. Music was evolving, and we were too. Jason Williams and I had Soundgarden, *Maggie's Dream and* Jane's Addiction, *plus all the wild metal and thrash we grew up on in the '80s like* Slayer *and* Voivod.

Do you remember other bands in the Rockford scene at the time? Was Sarkoma around then?

Rockford actually had a thriving music scene back in '89-'90. We gigged with many fine metal/thrash/punk acts from the area, with the Sarkoma *boys at the top of the heap.*

There were a lot of bands playing back then doing everything from punk to metal. You had Pinewood Box & Bludgeoned Nun to Mirrored Image and Ript to Diamond Force. Was there a lot of camaraderie among these varied bands or just the opposite?

There was a certain camaraderie among the members of the local acts even though we were very different stylistically.

I, personally, was accepted by the locals, and grew fond of many Rockford area bands such as Sarkoma, Ript, *and* Last Crack.

Who were the "go to" bands of Mirrored Image / For Christ Sake back in the day if you were looking to party? How wild did those parties get, I've heard stories. Can you relate any experiences?

If the parties got wild, it was William's (editor's note: lead singer Jason Williams) *crazy ass usually leading the festivities. Boy ain't right. I had the best years of my life hanging with that cat!*

I have a huge record collection, and during parties Jason would grab an album he hated, probably Lynyrd Skynyrd *or something, and ask if he could smash it! So we thinned out my records that way.*

There were always strippers and whiskey around the seemingly daily parties at the 4th Ave house (you were there). I spent many a hungover morning reassembling our furniture after Jason flatbacked it!

Why the name change? Was that '89?

We changed the name back in '91. We were looking to broaden our horizons regionally and nationally, and Mirrored Image seemed like a name for a local band. The way we changed our name was unique also.

We did it in the middle of one of our shows. We abruptly stopped in the middle of our set, had Brian Carter, singer of **Sarkoma**, *announce the name change to Forchristsake, dropped the new banner, and were off!*

"*On our way to play the Musicwest fest in Vancouver, we stayed over in Victor, Montana @ Mike William's place...awesome big country.*"

At what point did you start thinking that forchristsake had a real shot at being bigger than just a local Rockford band. What was the turning point for the band?

I think the turning point for FCS, and more and more bands regionally and nationally, was the evolving styles of music rock bands encountered in the early '90's.

Rock was reinventing itself (again), and we thought we could change the world. We were cock-sure that our signing with Gary Taylor and Re: Talent *would lead to big things.*

Prior to hooking up with your future manager was the band playing steadily around the Midwest or just the Northern IL area?

We played mostly regionally -- Rockford, Chicago, Madison, Milwaukee.

Tell me about finding your infamous future manager Gary Taylor. Who found who initially and how?

Mossy had a friend who worked for Gary Taylor, laid a tape on him, next thing he was in our funky-ass Rockford apartment offering to sign us.
Now this was huge for us, as Gary was already managing Annihilator *from Canada and* Last Crack *out of*

Madison. Both bands were touring the world, had videos on MTV...

And was he the force behind getting you guys on tour through the Pacific Northwest?
    I know you had a show booked in Vancouver, was that with Caustic Thought of at the time or was that where your manager was from?

    Yeah Gary managed Caustic Thought *too, and they were all from Vancouver B.C. We toured with* Caustic *up the west coast of the U.S. and into Vancouver. We also used to play with* Caustic *and* Last Crack *at CBGB's in New York frequently.*

Speaking of Caustic Thought, that was the band Byron Stroud and Devin Townshend were in prior to Strapping Young Lad, Fear Factory, Zimmer's Hole, etc.
    I remember the time they were staying with you guys in Rockford for a short time, thinking '92 time frame or thereabouts. Any stories / experiences you can relate? You still stay in touch with any of them?

    I remember the Canadians hated the low-quality weed in the Midwest. Devin Townsend was a trip, man. He was on the first west coast tour when he played with Caustic Thought. *That boy ain't right, either.*
    He went on tour with only the clothes on his back, his guitar and amp. No money, no spare clothes. His socks weren't allowed in the van, so he tied them to the side mirrors while we traveled.
    We were shown a great time while with Caustic, *especially in Vancouver, where the best strip clubs are located.*

Was it around this time that you guys shot that pro video for one of your songs? Whose idea was that, it had to be expensive. Was the intent to submit it to MTV? Was it submitted?

Well, our lady friends from "KitKat Clubs" in Rockford paid for the video. We struck a cool deal with Kundalini films out of Chicago and shot a video we hoped would be good enough to release, but it never saw the air.

Where were the live scenes shot?

We shot all the live stuff at the Times theatre *in Rockford. The video is posted on the Forchristsake Facebook page.*

Fast forward towards the end of FCS as a band. After the shit hit the fan with the manager, etc., how long did it take you to

93

move on musically or did you feel like you wanted OUT of music?

I did feel a break was needed. I'd never missed a rehearsal or gig in 12 years, and was going to take a year off, but my good friend, and last forchristsake drummer Bunj wouldn't have it.
He made me jam, and we formed our next band, Fluid OZ.

So where does everyone go and what do they do post FCS?

Everybody joined or formed important local and regional acts. Jason Williams sang in the infamous Motormouth, *then he joined* Agent Zero *for a few years. Mossy formed and toured with* The Heavils, *and is still making music today with his band* Staggg.

How many years did it take to get FCS back together and do the reunion shows?

We finally were able to pull it together in 2010 for one successful reunion show at the Back Bar *in Janesville.*

94

Are there more plans for more reunions shows?

You know, they're fun, but I really don't feel the need for any more shows. Jason lives in AZ now, so...
What about the following venues, can you talk about them, any memories you can share?

T.A. Verns – Milwaukee – I've had a few drinks there, don't remember so it must have been fun. Never played there.

Headliners – Madison – *Never played there, but was the place to catch all the up and coming metal act before they became big. I mean, we saw* Metallica *there on the "Ride the Lightning" tour. Front row, still have my Hetfield pick! Others acts I saw there before they got huge:* Soundgarden *(Kim Thayil and Chris Cornell had a guitar volume war on stage so it was the loudest show besides Motorhead I ever heard). Also,* W.A.S.P *(I was 12 inches from Blackies saw blade cod piece),* Krokus, Raven *and* Voivod.

Wally Gators – Madison – Awesome venue to get close to your heroes! Saw Vio-lence, and Voivod with all original members! Never played there.

O'Cayz Corral – Madison – *Probably the coolest dive bar I ever played besides CBGBs. Used to see the coolest acts there before they got big. My favorite show I saw there was the Veldt with 24-7 Spyz! These brothers can rock for sure.*

My band, forchristsake, played over half dozen shows at O'Cayz. The one show everybody remembers is the infamous show where Jason Williams, our singer, and I broke out the wall onstage during our set and spilled out on the sidewalk! Just the other day somebody filled me in on the details.

Allegedly, I was bouncing into the stage right wall which led to the entrance of the club, loosening up the wood for Jason to make the final plunge through. So, in the middle of a song, out he went, so I thought why not, and flew through the opening right behind him with my still plugged in bass, where I proceeded to fling my bass upside down across the busy street in front of O'Cayz! No cars hit it surprisingly.

I drug it by the guitar cable back to me, jumped back into the bar through the hole and continued playing. I'm sure it sounded great inside the bar. I don't remember if we were kicked out. Sure we didn't get paid. I just found out earlier this year that O'Cayz burned down way back when. Damn.

The County Line, City Limits, The Pier – Beloit – *Never played these venues. Used to drink in Beloit and Monroe Wisconsin as they were 18 yr old and over when Illinois was 21. So back in the late 70's, early 80's Beloit was the place for girls, booze and hard rock.*

Hard Times – Rockford – *Another scuzzhole forchristsake used to annihilate. Nasty, booze-soaked piss joint! We fucking rocked hard there, knowing we could cause no further damage.*

I remember playing a Halloween show there with forchristsake, *and my costume was a dead Greg DeCarlo, guitarist for the legendary Rockford rockers,* RIPT. *Usually this would have bought you an ass-beating, but for some reason, the* RIPT *clan were cool with it, and we've been buds ever since.*

Hurricane Harry's – Rockford – *Another dive bar, notorious for its odor. All the Rockford heavies played there in the early 90's.* forchristsake *played there with the* Sarkoma boys, N.I.L.8, *among others.*

Reflections – Rockford – *Never played there that I can remember, but we went there for the women. Used to go pussy-hunting with* forchristsake's *singer, Jason Williams here. Yes, Jason was quite the cocksman at Reflections.*

I never remember paying for a drink there either, but

always had a cocktail in my hand. It became our tradition to smash our empty drink glasses on the ground after every drink. I think we only were thrown out a few times.

The Loft – Freeport – *My hometown. This was back in '84-'85. I was playing bass in Lethal Heathen then, and we were much too metal (for the times) to be allowed to play clubs, but I remember seeing* Raven Bitch *there a few times. (Local heavy acts,* Raven Bitch, *along with* Last Crack *and* Ript *shoulda been huge.)*

Endless Nights – Rockford – *The last, best music venue Rockford ever had (closed in the early 90's). This was the place, if you were a Rockford area band, you wanted to play! Pro stage, righteous backstage, girls, plus Bruce Hammond did a fabulous job booking the place.*

Saw E'Nuff Z'Nuff *and* Cheap Trick *there. Sadly, I missed the* Mother Love Bone *show there in '89, '90. What a bummer!! Where I started my music career in Rockford. Where I played my first gig with* forchristsake *(we were called Mirrored Image then).*

If we weren't playing Endless Nights, me and Jason would be there partying. Used to go through the entrance, sling my leather across the room into the corner, drink all night, and my jacket would still be laying there in the corner.

Was accused of stealing beer, and selling or doing blow there, but I did neither. Used to hassle Bun E. Carlos at the bar all the time. He'd buy me a shot; I think to shut me up. Sorry Bun!

What about local music today?

There is no scene in Rockford. And if anyone tells you there is, they weren't around for the 80's or early 90's when Rockford still rocked. There's a handful of musicians doing awesome stuff in Rockford, but the venues to showcase local bands is limited to only Kryptonite and Mary's, if you're playing original music.

I trust the younger generation are in the garages and basements in Rockford, creating the next new thing, (I know they are...) waiting for some forward-thinking person to open up another club to give the kids a chance like I was given 30 years ago.

Locally the only real scene for local original bands is still Madison, Wisconsin. My current band, Vanishing Kids, have played to rousing success at the Frequency, Mickey's Tap, and High Noon Saloon in Madison. Madison still rocks!

What are you doing today, what's your life like now? Any Facebook pages or websites you'd like to plug?

Still at it, Theron. I play bass for Vanishing Kids. *Based in Madison, Nikki is such a talented vocalist and inspiring songwriter.*
Along with her husband, and equally talented guitarist, Jason Hartman, I feel the band could make some noise in the current scene.
Terry Nugent, drummer for my first band White Knight *(1982-83), plays for us too, so I'm kinda in a great situation currently.*

Vanishing Kids Facebook:
https://www.facebook.com/pages/Vanishing-Kids/328568887984

forchristsake Facebook:
https://www.facebook.com/pages/forchristsake/368543023754

Listen to forchristsake here:
http://www.last.fm/music/Forchristsake?ac=forchristsake

Spirit Visions, by V A N I S H I N G K I D S
vanishingkids.bandcamp.com

FOR CHRIST'S SAKE

Written by Amber Carroll

CLOSET ROCK, VANCOUVER, 1992

When I went to the Rock Cellar on the night of June 6th I wasn't really expecting to see much of anything interesting. My sole intention that Saturday night was to get real damn hammered off the Jack Daniels.

What happened instead? - FOR CHRIST'S SAKE!!!

Something happened from the minute they started their set. I can't even explain what it was that captivated me almost immediately and held my attention throughout their entire set - this happens very rarely when I'm only out to drink.

Even when some friends approached me in the club, I sent them off and asked them to catch me when FOR CHRIST'S SAKE finished their set.

What was so great about it? At the time I couldn't figure it out. There was no planned effects and nothing flashy going on up there. And these guys are definitely no pretty boy posers. In fact if anything they were klutzes - getting tangled up in each others equipment and ending up in a heap on the floor. Although this all appeared to be happening to the singer's dismay, I have to wonder...was it all in the plans guys?

Whatever the case, FOR CHRIST'S SAKE ended up winning the crowd over as their set progressed. I admit I was choked with the audience at first. It was obvious that everyone else in the club was only out to get smashed as well.

I felt like reaching out to all the other obnoxious drunks, choking them fuckin'

silly and screaming "YOU FUCKIN' IDIOTS! WAKE UP - OPEN YOUR EYES - LOOK AT THE STAGE! THESE GUYS ARE ACTUALLY TALENTED AND YOU'RE TOO BLOODY BUSY GETTING HAMMERED TO REALIZE THAT THERE'S SOME HUGE POTENTIAL UP THERE!!"

Fortunately I didn't do this, and eventually I didn't have to because the band pulled the crowd's attention in themselves. By the end of their set all the people that I wanted to commit brutal murder upon were actually banging their heads and totally intrigued. Needless to say, a huge smile came across my face as I felt the band had won some huge battle and emerged victorious. (Boy, I get carried away sometimes.)

Obviously I couldn't let these guys get away and head back home to Rockford, Illinois without getting a demo from them. I was so disappointed to find out that I would have to wait to reach them back in Illinois to get a package. Well, I finally recieved it and it was more than well worth the wait. In fact, in the process of getting their bio I got another surprise as well...FOR CHRIST'S SAKE are signed to a management agreement with one of Vancouver's well-known managers Gary Taylor(in the past Gary has worked with the likes of LAST CRACK and ANNIHILATOR and is currently managing CAUSTIC THOUGHT as well.)

O.K., so I haven't described the sound of the band yet. That's because I feel a quote from their bio package explains it so much better than I could ever put into words. However, I just want to mention that although the

following quote describes the band perfectly, I would have to warn one not to take the comparisons to seem that they are just another band jumping on the Seattle bandwagon.

If I were forced to compare them to another band (simply because people always feel the need to compare others to those of more popularity), I would not be able to pinpoint it. I myself could probably name about ten bands who's influences 'seem' to appear in their music which, if you think about it, makes them unlike any of the rest of them and uniquely FOR CHRIST'S SAKE!

Anyway, on with the quote...

"Imagine PEARL JAM meets JANE'S ADDICTION meets SOUNDGARDEN. Metal absolutely in sync with the incredibly successful Seattle sound and with the onslaught of Metallica's breakthrough. Lead vocalist Jason Williams is metal's spit in the face of Mariah Carey, a soaring voice that handles upper registers with such ease he makes Robert Plant sound like one of the Oak Ridge Boys (ed. - so true). Lead guitarist Ted Jacobi is a new guitar hero combining magic speed thrash with majestic ethereal lead excursions that jack the listener into outer space and pull him back down to earth with the gut-wrenching power of a crashing jet. The three-man rythm section--rythm guitarist Jason Vaughn, bassist Jerry Sofran and drummer Mike Wallace--are adept at all headbanging styles from ponderous sinister dredging to adrenaline-seizure teeth-grinding frenzy."
LES WISEMAN
Vancouver Magazine / TV Guide

••

Ray Horstheimer
Bugzy Malone

If you were into the Rockford hard rock / metal scene back in the 80's you knew about Bugzy Malone. They gigged so frequently that it was unusual <u>to not</u> hear their name or <u>not see</u> their flyers posted around town. Bugzy was the total package with the looks, the attitude, the stage presence and the music.

Their live performances were tight and in control. I can't say this about too many bands but they could've held their own with any national act of the day at a moment's notice. I'm proud to say I saw them twice. Once at *"The Cherry Lounge"* and the final time at the *"Midwest Jamfest."*

I had the pleasure to speak to Ray Horstmeier, bassist and founding member of this band. Ray's an amazing guy and this interview is everything I thought it would be and more. His insights into Bugzy as well as the local music scene of the 80's / 90's are extraordinary and really paint a vivid picture of the scene many of us once knew.

Give me the rundown on Bugzy Malone. What years was the band active?

Bugzy Malone was active from late in 1988 to 1991. Bugzy initially started in 1985 as Rock City and stayed with that name until 1987. After Rock City ended we made a couple of changes and formed Bugzy Malone. The three core members remained for the entire duration from 1985 through 1991.

Bugzy Malone

Appearing At
Cherry Lounge
June 9th, 10th
8:00

Dell School Rd.
Behind Cherryvale

Lenny "Jetta" LaSalle
Billy Ray Rivers
Staci Heartless
Johnny Fish

What were the expectations for Bugzy? Gig around as a local band, have fun, or pursue it as a career?

This whole thing started with a guitarist friend and I jamming along to cassettes of AC/DC, Iron Maiden, Rush, Dio *and of course* Grim Reaper. *It wasn't long before a friend of a friend started drumming; Johnny Fish found out from our parents talking that we were jamming and started playing guitar with us. The final piece of this was a friend of mine joining us on vocals.*

The only intention we had at first was just jamming together, of course this all changed when someone suggested we play for a party they were having. One party was all it took and we wanted to play anywhere and everywhere as long as it was an outdoor party.

When Rock City dried up, we started Bugzy Malone. *Steve, Johnny and I really wanted the style of Bugzy to reflect our personalities and influences as well as being different from anything in our local area. It also dawned on us that we might want to look at playing clubs instead of just parties and also writing our own music.*

Where we grew up we really had no type of direction from anyone as how to go about this so we did the best we could with the resources we had. I remember getting our first club gig as Bugzy at the Cherry Lounge and thought we were really on our way.

That idea even became more pronounced when Mike from Ript *called and wanted to know if we would be interested in doing a three night run with them at Tinkers Lounge. Of course we accepted and I think at this point we may have started to think we would love to be able to do this for a living, after all we were now playing with bands we respected and never imagined we would share a stage with some of these bands.*

Looking back on that scene, do you think Northern IL had a shot at becoming the next "Sunset Strip" in terms of metal?

Possibly with the talent in the area, the music some of these local bands were writing and the clubs that were around, it could have happened if it wasn't such a logistical nightmare. I mean Chicago had the busiest airport in the world at that time and there were not musicians flocking to Chicago either.

There were so many musicians with a diversity of styles in Rockford that I really respected and loved watching play. You could go to a club any night of the week and see a great band. I think the weather, the atmosphere and the all-around history of the west coast kind of sealed the deal for them as being the place to be. I also couldn't really see people flocking to Rockford in January to get their big break while having to sleep in their cars and tote their gear in subzero temperatures.

There were quite a few bands that were on the *"edge"* in terms of really breaking out and maybe becoming national acts like forchristsake, Ript, Sarkoma and even you guys. Is this some kind of Rockford curse? Why didn't this happen?

I really don't think there is a Rockford curse, I think it is the Midwest in general. Everything seems to happen first on either coast and that is where the trends first start.

By the time the momentum of that trend makes its way to the Midwest there is already something new starting on either coast. In the late 80's to early 90's there was not the information at our fingertips 24/7 like there is today. Most of what we knew about that was happening in the music world was through MTV and rock magazines. By the time Midwest bands started to gain momentum and catch on, the musical landscape was already changing and we found ourselves on the tail end.

I was living in Minneapolis in the early 90's and remember Ript coming through on the last stop of the tour they were on. They were playing a really cool club called the "Mirage." I was excited to see Ript in a club like the Mirage and I hadn't seen those guys in a while. What a disappointment it was when there was only 30 people in a huge club like that for a band like Ript. At that point I just knew that change, and not change I was happy to see, was on its way.

Bugzy did a show case at TA Verns with Hericane Alice, tell me about that, and was there label interest in you guys?

I really don't know if there was label interest in Bugzy, there may have been just a tiny bit in 1989. After we played the Midwest Jamfest we were approached about playing a show at TA Verns in Milwaukee with Hurricane Alice and Megaton Blonde for reps from Atlantic Records.

105

I think at that time they were still spelling the name as "Hurricane Alice." Of course we were not going to turn that kind of an opportunity down. Of all the clubs on my list to play, TA Verns was at the top.

I remember that place being packed on both floors and of course when we took the stage there was a group of guys on my side of the stage screaming every name they could come up with pertaining to guys in make up with big hair and leather clothes. Thank God they got booted by some people that wanted to see us.

Of course while this was going on I was trying to move to the guitarist's side of the stage so I didn't have to listen to it, but those guitarists aren't going to let anyone on their little piece of real estate! Lol. All in all, that was a fun show and a great experience.

Why not pack it up and move to LA instead of sticking around Rockford?

A couple of our members really considered moving to LA but changed their mind. I think not packing it up goes hand in hand with my earlier statements about trends. If you move around chasing trends you will always be on the end of it.
There is probably just as good of a chance of staying put, doing your thing and letting the cycle come back around. The percentage of people that actually made it by moving west can't be that high. I have had a pretty damn good life because I stayed here and I doubt if that would have happened if I took my chances and went west.

Had you done that, moved the band to LA, do you think you could've been signed?

I really don't know; some people like to think we would have. I have always been positive but I have also always been a realist. If we would have got signed I think we would have been a mid-level band that didn't do much more than clubs and possibly an opening slot on a small tour. There was really some good music that Steve and Johnny wrote but I don't know if we could have translated that to the bigger picture at the time.
My whole basis for this comes from seeing Warrant *open for* D'Molls *at Endless Nights on State and Madison in what had to be late 1988 or early 1989.* D'Molls *was supposed to be the next big thing and* Warrant *was just signed.* Warrant *had to be one of the best bands I had ever seen in that kind of a setting and completely kicked* D'Molls *ass off the stage.*
We went there to see D'Molls *and had never heard of* Warrant, *There were only about 20 people in the club that night and we got a table up front. Warrant came out and their first song, Jani was already dancing on our table, all*

107

over the room and just had this enormous presence. Their set was practically flawless!

The only thing the guy I was with could say for the next week was how Warrant *was going to be huge! Sure enough, a month later and* Warrant *was opening for* Motley Crue *on the Dr Feelgood tour. After seeing that Warrant show at Endless Nights and then seeing them on the* Motley *tour, I just couldn't see how many bands could compete with that.*

The whole Jani Lane story and his death still bugs me. I saw this guy at the beginning of his career and saw how much charisma, talent and character he had, he was so up and full of life. Then watching him spiral down over the years even though he attained the kind of success most of us only dream about.

I spoke with him for a while that night at Endless Nights and a couple times over the years; he was just such a down to earth guy that still had that enormous presence even though he wasn't all that happy.

Did the band do gigs outside of Northern IL, did you ever tour at all?

Just Illinois and Wisconsin, we could have played every night if we wanted too.

At what point, as well as year, did the band come to an end and why? Were there any signs that Bugzy was coming to an end or did it just happen?

Bugzy ended in 1991, I don't really remember how it ended, we were all just getting tired of it and needed to do something else. We spent practically 7 days a week for 7 years doing nothing but music.

Was it an amicable split in terms of the band ending or was it ugly?

I don't remember it being an ugly split at all. There were some Sundays we would still get together after we split, head to a local creek, go crayfishing, then bring them back to my place for a crayfish boil. Of course we always ended up at the local bar having cheeseburgers because eating those little crayfish was more work than they were filling.

Has there been talk about a reunion at all, maybe recently?

We did a reunion show about 10 years ago for a friend's birthday and that has really been it. There are people that ask us frequently if we will ever do another show but at this point it is highly unlikely.

Looking back on the scene now, any change of heart, do you think it was as strong and good as you remember?

I really think it was a strong music scene. As I said earlier there were so many great bands and such diversity. It seemed the bands at that time were really living the music, that lifestyle, and believing they had something great to offer, not just getting up on stage and going through the motions.

What's your take on hard rock / metal nowadays, still good or not?

I still like rock and metal and will until the day I die. The music scene as a whole is so saturated. There are not many bands today that have a lot of staying power and I think that is unfortunately due to our society needing instant gratification. No one will wait three years anymore for a new release and tour.

What's the post band breakup story now? Where's everyone at, what are they doing and are you still playing music?

Everyone is doing well and I know where everyone is located. We don't really keep in touch or talk that often but I still think of those guys every day. I am working for a fortune 200 company and staying busy with projects around our property. My wife and I have also been extremely busy with family and keeping up with the grandkids.
Add my passion of restoring vintage Kawasaki snowmobiles and old cars to the mix and I really don't have the time for playing. I don't really have the passion and drive either anymore for what it takes to keep a band rolling. I will always have a passion for music and the utmost respect for the guys I know still busting their butts in the music industry.
I have filled in for a friend's bands in Minneapolis on occasion but that is really it for music. Although I do have a small two-man show coming up in the near future with Kris

from Hairball. *I have known him a long time and it will feel good to spend some time playing music with him again.*

Thanks for giving me the opportunity to fill people in on how I remember those days 20 some years ago and thanks for keeping the flag flying for old school musicians!

Paul Bronson
Zanthus

How did Zanthus happen? Did you always want to be a musician; did you have friends in other local bands that inspired you?

Paul Bronson: *Zanthus was founded in 1985/1986 by former members of the Rockford area band Stormhouse/Sativa: Paul Bronson and Tim Gargani. I always wanted to play in a band but as a profession, not as serious as some others in the Rockford area.*

How long was the band around?

1985 - 1992

What eventually ended Zanthus? Did you see the demise of the band coming or did it surprise you?

Tim Gargani actually left the band in 1992 and that was the end of the era. I did not see it coming. Tim said he wanted to do something "different" ... He went on to join Stronghold another Rockford-area band.

Any hard feelings looking back at Zanthus, or, is it all water under the bridge at this point?

You can't live in the past with anything really in life. The future is what matters because that is the only thing you can have an effect on.

Was there a feeling that Rockford's hard rock / metal scene of the 80's / 90's was one of the stronger ones in the Midwest and maybe it could garner some kind of national spotlight? Think it ever had the chance of becoming, say, the next "Sunset Strip?"

I don't know about being compared to an LA music scene, so many rose to become international stars. There was an incredible amount of great hard rock/metal bands at that point in time for sure.

What was the band's outlook like back then, were you playing just for fun or did you have intentions of making it a full time gig?

I was doing it more out of my love for playing music more than anything. Still do. As far as full-time aspirations, I was pretty grounded with my head. My parents always told me to "make sure you have something to fall back on".
Are there any demos / records that Zanthus did?

YES!! We did an EP in January 1991 at the Noise Chamber in Loves Park, IL. Jimmy Johnson produced those sessions and it STILL holds up to this day as great recordings.

Zanthus, Cherry Lounge, 1987

I'll mention some venues and plz give me your best recollections of them whether you played them or just hung at them:

Stars 100 – Milwaukee - *Played there once with High Treason*

The Haven – Milwaukee - *Zanthus did 3-4 shows in 1991/92 bad ass sound system*

The County Line – Beloit - *Used to hang out there in the early 80's a bit*

City Limits – Beloit - *Used to go there ALL the time. Peter Lorre/ Bittersweet*

The Pier – Beloit – *Used to hang out there a few times.*

Hard Times – Rockford – *Zanthus never played there but I was there A LOT!!*

Hurricane Harrys – Rockford - *Zanthus played there quite a bit – nasty carpets!*

Reflections – Rockford – *The scene of the final Zanthus show in June 1992. Great place to play \m/*
The Loft – Freeport - *Never played there*

All these years later, how do you remember Rockford's hard rock / metal scene back then? Was it as dynamic and exciting as you recall it?

It was exciting for sure. The lack of band comradery really sucked. There was a lot animosity instead of support.

115

Was there any talk of Zanthus touring, say the Midwest? Was there ever any talk of maybe a bunch of local bands, Zanthus included, touring as a package show?

We never really got that far into it. Seemed like the members came and went too frequently to solidify a unit that could go on a mini-tour.

What are you up today and are you still playing music?

I am. I am in the Rockford-area hard rock/metal cover band PULSE18. We are actually covering a couple songs that Zanthus did back in the day. It is mostly never hard rock/metal ala WXRX & WJJO playlists. I also do solo acoustic instrumental shows frequently in the Rockford area. I'm also working on releasing a CD of my original solo acoustic instrumental pieces. That should be available by end of summer 2015.

Dave Potter
Music / Program Director
WYBR

What years were you with WYBR? Were you an on air personality or program director? Where did you come from prior to WYBR?

Dave Potter: *1987-1989 – I joined the team as a weekend overnighter- playing the pre-recorded Beatle Years and "FlashBack" programs, doing the weather, managing the AM auto-feeds, etc. – the music director at the time was leaving, so when he left – I took over his spot, as well, the program director – Jeff Manning left 6 months later – so I adopted both roles.*
  Keep in mind, one month before I started there – North-star Broadcasting Group decided to sell the station - a process that takes one year to put up for sale, then countless months to process... so we were in "who cares, let's try this" mode the whole time. Previous to the station, I was DJ'ing around town, including a steady gig as half-DJ / half-Bar Manager at the downtown club "Oscars."

Had you promoted concerts through the radio station prior to the Midwest Jamfest? If so, which ones were they and are there any stories you can tell re: meeting various bands or rock stars?

  As part of my role, I was handling all the label communications, music programming and playlist reporting to Radio & Records – so any concert that came to Rockford, and through WYBR – I arranged; with the help obviously of whatever label rep was pushing that band through their tour.

While we saw a good band here in Rockford once or twice every couple of months, I was in Chicago 3-5 nights a week seeing even more acts on the labels dime. (That's how the reps got Music Directors to play the singles when they were released, and in turn report that play to R&R.)

![Y95 The Rock Station Rockford & Disc Records welcome]

Were you involved in any of the *"Hometown Heroes"* records? Do you know how that came about and how the bands were chosen for them?

Hometown Heroes was a product of Jeff Manning and some local band promotions guys – I literally created the display for that album at Appletree from scratch in my garage – because marketing wasn't planned / paid for very well – I didn't continue that program the following year because I couldn't find any support for it (the station wasn't going to flip the bill as they did the past few years).

Looking back on your time at the station in the 80's / 90's, was Rockford radio, FM rock / pop radio, was it firing on all cylinders or did it miss the mark? How could it have been better?

I say this: Rockford Radio has had its heroes, I mean, Y95 was by far and to this day, the best station I've ever known – but they were a product of the seventies; when DJs had actual control, and the sales guys didn't have to make a quota to cover the bills.

Once the record labels started getting slapped on the hands for "courting" the stations and covering nights of sex, drugs and rock n' roll for the radio station's personnel, all of the sudden these partiers had to find more income at the air-time level.

I wasn't into ZOK much, it had already become too much bubblegum by the mid 80's, but I'm proud of the experimentation we did at WYBR, we went from number 7 to number 2 during the sales process – wish I had been there sooner. Maybe there's a lesson about loosening the reigns there somewhere, right?

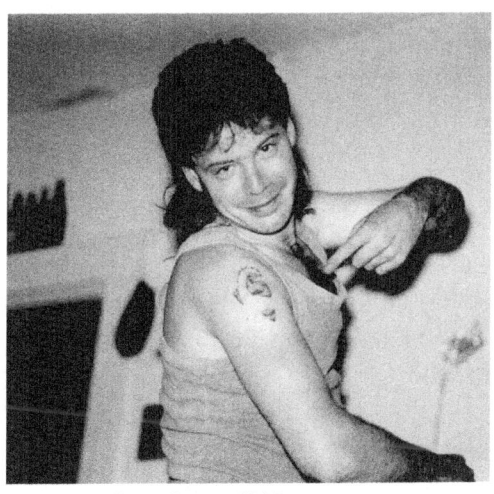

Dave Potter, 1990

Was the radio station playing local music on air while you were there? If so, who was championing that, do you remember?

Rich Gordon, although mostly the local Blues scene, he was all over the locals (he still is – love that guy!) – We saw a fair share of efforts here and there on other stuff, I remember doing a Sunday afternoon thing with the daytime chick (name escapes me, Jade?) – That concentrated on alternative AND local flavor – think it lasted 6 months, we couldn't sell enough commercials for it.

Did you find Rockford media in general to be supportive of the local arts and local music back then? Or was is it ignored, maybe they didn't clue in to it?

I'm not going to have a good thing to say about the Rockford Media – with the recent demise of "On the Waterfront," and the hard time that "Transform Rockford" is having getting people to give a shit.
I'd say that they're one of the main culprits for not committing to the Rockford scene, like ever. The people in Rockford who you see trying hard, are killing themselves to get support.

Outside of work were you involved with the local music scene at all? Did you know the bands, go to any shows? If so who were the bands you were following back then? Still in touch with them now?

I've always been an alternative guy. I listen to everything – always have – but alternative, punk and new wave have always been at the top. So naturally, I'm going to mention Pinewood Box *as one of my favs, and yes – still talk to Rainwater and Scary Dan every once in a while. I kinda hung out with a few others back then,* RIPT, *etc. But the* Pinewood *guys were from my click.*

Looking back on that scene, do you think Northern IL ever had a shot at becoming the next hot bed for music, the next nationally recognized place like say, Hollywood or Seattle?

Not a chance, its proximity to Chicago would always overshadow them. It's unfortunate though, because growing up here, Rockford's rural youth and the lifestyle led always seemed like the perfect catalyst to become stellar or famously rebellious – just too much competition from the East.

There were quite a few bands that were on the "edge" in terms of really breaking out and maybe becoming national acts. So many bands, why do you think it didn't happen?

#9, once a band got close – they were at the mercy of the labels reps – who lived, worked, and "played" in downtown Chicago – their attention and effort to support bands from, at that time, "too far away" was too hard to maintain and pay for.

Looking back on the 80's even the 90's local music scene (hard rock, metal, etc.), was it as strong and dynamic as you remember it or if not, how do you remember it?

It was crazy strong from my perspective, even now. We really did have a lot of bands going, creating and hitting the stages in droves. While I'm disappointed more of them didn't make it further – you can't tell me they didn't have an influence on what us spectators did later – I still judge some of my successes and failures on how the world seemed then – some of the most influential parts of my life.

Do you still live in the area? If you do, do you still follow local music? Is it as good or better than it was back then? If so, why?

I do still live close, but not in Rockford. I'm there all the time for work and I'm back donating time and effort to the Rockford Art Museum. My friends and I still get out to see the bands, although it was easier with things like the "GrooveWalk" and "...Waterfront."

We've started to frequent the City Market thing and hope to see more of that. I don't think I see as much as I remember it being back then but I do see quality in what's being done for sure. I enjoy knowing folks like Bruce Hammond and the like are still going at it – it's a kick for sure.

How do you look at rock music now as an adult and not a kid? Do you see it differently; do you see flaws in it or is it just as great as ever?

I'm consistently disappointed with the present mainstream music scene – but locally, I'm optimistic about the future.

What are you doing today? Still in radio. Tell me about life post WYBR.

Radio fell into my lap, I loved it then, but it cost me a very important relationship (too many long nights in

122

Chicago) and a lot of lost sleep. I did consult / create playlists for stations in St. Louis and Baltimore for a few months after the new owners (WXRX) "let me go" – but it wasn't the same.

I went back to my passion in graphic design and presently direct business development for a company out of Chicago as well as consult manufacturers around the country with their marketing efforts.

After 28 years – I managed to get that same relationship back; she'd kill me if I started radio again. ☺

MIDWEST JAMFEST
Ace of Diamonds Club, 1989

Poster from the collection of Mossy Vaughn

Dave Potter
Y95 Music / Program Director
Organizer, Midwest Jamfest, 1989
Ace of Diamonds Club, Rockford IL

From the collection of Ronald Keinz

Tell me about the Midwest Jamfest, its origins and how it went. I was there. I remember it being very hot and cold beer was about the only thing that would cool you off that day.

It began as a simple benefit for a local kid who had some form of Leukemia – not as prevalent back then as now. The owner of the club "Ace of Diamonds" came to me with it and while initially the station hated the idea, in the end they supported it.

I managed to scrape up enough volunteers to help, although I believe I was unable to move for a few days after that from all the work. In the end, we had to shut down before the headliner came on due to some old lady in Gem Suburban who thought it was too loud – but Enuff Z'nuff *was very understanding and still partied as if they had performed – at a local hotel (damages, wow!).*

But a few days later I realized how many bands played, and how big the crowd was and felt pretty awesome about it all. Financially, we were able to contribute to the kid's family – but not near as much as we had hoped.

Do you think it could've gone better? Was it a good thing in the long run or not? How do you look back on it?

Again, I'm proud of it, it's one of those things that in my mind would have been awesome to continue, the rare errors in the way it was setup would've been easy to fix – I really feel it could have been something great if continued.

Would you do it over again? What would you do different?

I would if I could quit everything else I was doing and fully commit to it, I'd find corporate sponsors and not depend on a station, or the media.

Jerry Sofran
forchristsake / Mirrored Image

Ok, as I understand it, you weren't in a band just yet. You had just arrived in Rockford and here you are at the Midwest Jamfest. You ride in on your Harley. Take it from here if you could...

Yeah I was new to Rockford and was still riding the hog. Everybody was playing the Jam Fest including my future band, Mirrored Image. Rockford still had a thriving music scene back in '89, and I was about to enter into it.

All the local musicians welcome me with open arms (and bottles), and when I rolled in backstage on the Harley I got instant cred.

What brought you to Rockford and how did you hear of this event?

I am originally from Freeport, Illinois, and was going to San Francisco to join a real metal band, but my girlfriend got cold feet on the way, we stopped overnight at Mirrored Image's *singer Jason Williams place in Rockford, and ended up staying awhile.*

The Jam Fest was the place to be that day, probably heard about it in the R.A.M. MaGAZINE (Rockford Area Music), one of the local music rags around town.

Did you meet any bands that day, do some networking?

Christ Theron, I probably did. I can't remember. I got along with every band here in Rockford.

Is that the day that you joined Mirrored Image?

No, but was in the band less than a month after. I think this was Mirrored Image's last show with the old bassist.

Who were the stand out bands you saw? I remember Megaton Blonde killing it hard.

Wow...so long ago. Did Megaton Blonde *play it? They were huge in the 80's. Maybe* RIPT? *They were always my favorite locals. Should have been huge.*

Was much partying done on your part that day?

Not much. I didn't party while I rode so I'm sure I maintained.

The Midwest Jamfest was 1989. Since then Rockford had the annual WXRX Wing Ding fest at The Rockford Speedway which is no more. Why can't this town support a damn rock fest? Is it really that difficult?

Cuz Rockford. *There's probably more questions than answers on why this town has no scene. There's plenty of local fans, starving for entertainment. The few concerts in the area are usually well attended. Maybe the agents and people running the music venues are clueless. When's the last time there was anything decent at the MetroCentre? I think most touring acts making money skip Rockford. Once you've been a has-been for 20 years, then you play Rockford.*
Someone needs to give the bands with people 16-24 years old a chance to make some noise, then maybe the scene can be cool again. The young cats are the future of music. The little I've heard of new young bands has been amazing. I played a show with local act Tundras *and they rocked. The kids are alright.*

Mossy Vaughn
Mirrored Image

Do you remember how or who gave you the invite to perform at the Midwest Jamfest?

I think Jason Williams probably got the gig for us he was always "networking" at the bars...

I remember that day being hotter than hell and the backstage beer scene disappearing fast. What was your backstage experience like and what time did you guys on stage?

We went on early it was hot real hot. I remember when the beer ran out people were freaking out getting in cars and going for more.

> The first band that really got any reaction at all out of the comatose audience was the speed heavy **Mirrored Image**. They immediately grabbed the audience by the balls, pounding out a jarring set that made everyone take notice. Their sound had a Testament-like heaviness to it, packed with an impressive Laaz Rockit-Exodus punch.
>
> Highlights from their set included <u>Life</u> and Death Angel's <u>Bored</u>. Asked if the latter was a personal statement about the crowd, the band's lead singer Jason Williams responded by saying, "Death Angel is a favorite of ours, but (the crowd) must be bored. by be sitting down." When asked about the crowd showing he thought it was "a decent turnout, but as soon as it gets dark and everyone starts getting more drunk, it'll get better." Always the optimist. The band has plans to go back into the studio and crank out a new six song demo. Keep your eyes open for it - that'll be one nrk to miss.

Was there a lot of buzz for this event prior to it happening? Was it well advertised?

It was well advertised as far as I remember Y 95 always did a good job with that. But being so hot early in the day the crowd was thin until dusk.

Was there any motivation to get there early in the day and hang for the fest or arrive maybe an hour or so before your time slot to perform?

We usually got there early to party and hang out -- we like to party.

Hot day. Free beer disappearing fast. Were bands cool that day with one another or was there bullshit.

I don't remember anything weird happening. We always had a good time playing to 1 or 1000 people.

130

Which bands were you sandwiched in between, you remember?

No. Ript played "Babies in a Blender" and that got me going...

I don't remember a whole of merchandising going on that day. Was there any, did you guys do alright?

I don't think we had merch for this show.

How could the event have gone smoother, if at all?

More beer, more hairspray; there could of been trailers filled with stripper poles and small men in short shorts serving drinks and appetizers...

I know this was an Y95 sponsored event. It should've been an annual thing if not by Y95 then someone else organizing and promoting it. Why didn't it happen, this was during the heyday of Rockford's hard rock / metal scene?

I don't think many people have enough follow through...

Could an event of this type happen now in Rockford and succeed? If not, why?

Maybe, there is actually a scene again starting in Rockford, not just metal but a lot of diverse good bands playing original music. So yea I always believe...

Paul Bronson
Zanthus

Do you remember how or who gave you the invite to the Midwest Jamfest?

I do not. I believe Tim "Hollywood" Merwin (RIP) secured that gig?

I remember that day being hotter than hell and the backstage beer scene disappearing fast. What was your backstage experience like and what time did you guys on stage?

They had a tent off to the side of the entire stage area for all the bands with beer and pizza which kept being delivered as it ran out, for a while...

Was there a lot of buzz for this event prior to it happening? Was it well advertised?

No, I think it was not widely known it was even happening in the area until the week of the concert.

Was there any motivation to get there early in the day and hang for the fest or arrive maybe an hour or so before your time slot to perform?

Oh yeah, BEER!! LOL. We got there about 3 hours before our time slot and everything was running about 45 minutes behind schedule. Plenty of time for Gary Christiansen to get tanked. And he did. LOL.

Hot day. Free beer disappearing fast. Were bands cool that day with one another or was there bullshit.

I don't recall any bullshit between bands. But it was 1989, there was not the best comradery that today's Rockford music scene has.

Was it a good time or a bust?
Any time you get to play on a huge festival stage it's cool. Definitely poorly attended and poorly promoted.

Which bands were you sandwiched in between, you remember?

LOL... I don't recall

Which bands, per your recollection, were the stand outs that day, I mean, really played killer sets?

RIPT always delivered and Megaton Blond were on fire that day!

I don't remember a whole of merchandising going on that day. Was there any, did you guys do alright?

I don't recall any at that time either. We did not.

How could the event have gone smoother, if at all?

Promotion, Promotion, Promotion. People almost found about the concert after-the-fact...

I know this was an Y95 sponsored event. It should've been an annual thing if not by Y95 then someone else organizing and promoting it. Why didn't it happen, this was during the heyday of Rockford's hard rock / metal scene?

I have no idea why the 1st Annual Midwest Jamfest was the only annual LOL... Guess they lost enough money on the first one.

Could an event of this type happen now in Rockford and succeed? If not, why?

Absolutely it could. Wing Ding was a perennial thing for a while and that became a big event. It would be nice to see something like with 2-3 Nationals and the rest of the support from local bands.

135

Ray Horstheimer
Bugzy Malone

"Oh the infamous Midwest Jamfest! Dave Potter and WYBR put the thing together for a leukemia benefit. The whole premise and idea for that was great and I really don't know why it didn't have a better turnout. Enuff Znuff was getting big and they were supposed to be the headliner.

There were bands like Ript, Zanthus, Mirrored Image, Diamond Force and Right Mind on this bill and all of those bands had a lot of drawing power. Add Enuff Znuff to that list and there should have been one hell of a turnout. I don't know if it didn't do well because it was on a hot Sunday in August or there were just too many other things going on.

It was set up well and the budget for this had to be huge. There was a huge stage and PA, great lighting, alcohol and a VIP tent. They may have tried to get too many things to happen in one day. There was a laser show that had some problems with the airport being so close and a few other delays.

If I remember right, it was so hot that all the bands just hung back in the tent and ate and drank until it was time to go on. That was a great experience and I can still see Vern the number one local music fan spending the whole day in front of the stage wearing his blue suit on a humid 95-degree day. I think the program director may have lost his job due to this show."

Todd Houston
Midnite Angel

Before we get into talking about area venues, what bands were you in back in the 80's? And what got you into hard rock / metal in the first place?

Todd Houston: *The first band I was in worth mentioning was* Midnite Angel *around 1986 or 87. We were together until 1989 and then* Smack Street *followed.*

As far as getting into hard rock and metal, for me I suppose it was Kiss *and hearing Ace's lead guitar. When I finally got a guitar of my own I was baffled how he achieved that distorted tone and searing sustain! I knew nothing about distortion pedals and amplifiers let alone guitars.*

Were you ever of the mindset that you'd be a professional musician or was it always a hobby / weekend type thing to do?

They say ignorance is bliss and I believe it to be true. Having said that, yes, I also believed that being a rock star was very obtainable simply because nobody told me otherwise.

I later found out that I had tremendous anxiety and struggled with being onstage in front of people. I was okay as long as no one expected me to jump around too much! I really had to concentrate on what I was doing.

You curate the popular "Rockford Rocked" & "Rockford Area Bands Nostalgia" Facebook pages. How did that come about?

First off, I had had the idea for years. "Rockford Rocked" started out as a way for me to showcase area music from the past. I had a handful of photos and some audio from various local acts from the 70's and 80's but didn't know how to get it out there other than spending money and creating a website that might or might not be seen.

When Facebook came along I thought man, what a great vehicle to use for getting this stuff out to people! AND it's free! (Laughs). After a while "Rockford Rocked" became more of a "Rockford city history" page. I thought it was time to separate the two giving the music thing a home of its own.

Looking back at the Northern IL / Southern WI (including Milwaukee) hard rock / metal music scenes of the 80's and 90's, was it as strong and dynamic as you remember or not so, and why?

Yes. The Rockford area was full of hard rock/ metal bands during that time Theron. You have to remember that a lot of the popular MTV era music was very visual meaning there was an actual "show" to see. These local bands were spending most if not all of their payoff on fog machines, lights and giant P.A. systems.

As for our friends in Beloit, Janesville and Milwaukee, the same thing was happening. You had T.A. Verns, Headliners, Back of the Yards, The Haven, *etc. It was a way of life for a lot of folks. You looked the part on and offstage. Eyeliner, Hairspray, leather.*

These days we get to watch Mumford and Sons. *You can only wear 1920's garb in so many ways before eventually becoming a parody of yourselves and that's what finally happened to our crowd. Every dog has its day I suppose.*

Todd Houston, 1994

Looking back on it now, do you think Northern IL / Southern WI (including Milwaukee) had any chance of becoming the next breakout hard rock metal scene say, like, The Sunset Strip was in the 80's?

I don't think so and I'll tell you why. 1. This is the Midwest. 2. The Midwest is typically 3-4 years behind the West and East coasts. In other words, by the time a new trend hits us it's pretty much fizzled out in L.A. and New York. Record companies were already focusing on bands like Mudhoney and The Melvins when we were buying the new Skid Row release.

Who were the local bands from the Northern IL / Southern WI (including Milwaukee) hard rock / metal music scenes of the 80's and 90's we should talk about and remember?

There were a handful of quality bands out there doing it right. There are certain things that make me remember a band. One of the first things is attitude and the second is musicianship. If you happen to have both you're in the game. Moxy Roxx, Zanthus, Boneyard. RIPT, Megaton Blond, and Raven Bitch are just a few that stick out for me.

Looking at the current hard rock / metal scenes of Northern IL / Southern WI (including Milwaukee) is as good, better or worse than how it was back in the 80's / 90's?

I'm not really privy to speak about our good friends in Wisconsin but I'll tell you this, it really doesn't compare at all. Like I said before back then it was a way of life. Even if you weren't a musician, rock and metal were a way of life for a lot of folks.

The culture has changed so dramatically that I'm not sure there is even a scene to speak of anymore. Keep in mind that I am comparing it to the glory years of the 1980's. There have been a lot of peaks and valleys since then to be fair I suppose.

Ok. Time to talk about venues. Give me as much information, detail, memories, etc. about each one listed below and don't hold back. And if I missed a popular bar / club / venue that hosted hard rock / metal / alt / punk bands from the 80's, please include it as well.

City Limits – Beloit – I was too young to go there on a regular basis but I do recall that they were probably the busiest live music venue in Beloit at one time. They had live music there seven days a week for Pete's sake! Armed Vision, Jewels Blatner, Ruby Starr were all regulars. I am positive that some hearts were broken, some beer was consumed and some lives were changed forever at the City Limits.

The Pier – Beloit – The Pier was what a great rock club should be! It was dark, smelled like stale beer and had a cool stage. It was also where Moxy Roxx played when they were in Beloit most of the time. Never go to the Pier on quarter beer night in the middle of a raging snow storm on a Wednesday… just sayin.

Hard Times – Rockford – Hard Times was more of a rocker hang out than it was a live music venue although they did start hosting bands toward the end of their run. I remember the waitresses and bartenders were typically very easy on the eyes. It was a good place to find a drummer and have some chicken wings.

Hurricane Harrys – Rockford – As a band at the time were very excited to get a new place in Rockford to play. Hurricane Harry's caught the tail end of what was left of the rock culture in Rockford as far as I'm concerned. The word decadence comes to mind. What went on at Harry's stayed at Harry's along with the vomit smell and roaches.

Reflections – Rockford – For me Reflections was more of a place where different cliques could intermingle and buy each other drinks. I remember seeing Zanthus, ICU, Sarkoma and Pandemonium Circus there. To tell you the truth I liked it better on the nights that bands weren't playing as it was easier to talk to the girls… and trust me, there was no shortage of single girls at Reflections!

Of all the venues listed above, which one was a big favorite amongst hard rock / metal musicians and why?

I'm going to go with The City Limits at its peak! Iconic live music venue coupled with an iconic era for music!

The *"On The Waterfront"* festival was discontinued and Hard Times (formerly Stash O'Neils restaurant) recently made headlines when it was used as a marijuana grow facility. Yikes! What's happened to Rockford? Does the city not support local music and arts?

Look, here's the deal… OTWF was originally intended as a music festival. The rides were just a bonus. People stopped supporting the music, it annoyed them as they tried to stuff their faces with Elephant ears. Every year more stages were removed and kids with baggy pants took their place.

As far as Hard Times is concerned I plan on buying it and turning it into a museum. You can go there with your kids and look at the walls which will be filled with photos of Rockford musicians and iconic landmark venues. The jukebox will be nothing but local artists! Oh yeah, did I mention the craft beer?

Do you ever see a time again when the local Rockford music scene will ever be as strong as it was in the 80's, in terms of rock? What's gotta take place locally for this to happen?

No. When Gene Simmons said Rock is dead he wasn't too far off. What I really think he meant was "rock culture" is dead or it at least has a bad infection. Sorry, there will never be another era like it so stop holding your breath folks. Not in Rockford, not anywhere. Thankfully there are people like you and I to tell these stories.

Greg DeCarlo
RIPT

What year was RIPT started?

I believe RIPT was around '84, '85, and I didn't join the band till '88. So they would've been together three or four years prior to me. Ian and I joined right around the same time, mid-November of '88. Ian took over after Steve Moriarty left. There was tension between Steve and a few other guys in the band. Being in a band is like being in a relationship and it was just an incompatible situation. Compound it with high testosterone and lots of alcohol and there you go.

You guys all get along now?

Oh yeah, yeah. We all stay in touch as much as we can. Greg Utley travels alot, he's vice president of Bay Stage Lighting. One of the largest lighting companies in the US.

Via text message of Facebook we all stay in touch. I talk to Ringo a couple of times a month minimum. Myself and Wally are both here in Rockford. Ian is in Schaumburg, about an hour and a half from here, a suburb of Chicago. Mike, I think is in the St. Petersburg area, I'm not quite sure, I should know this, and Greg actually lives in St. Pete. I don't talk to Wally too much but I think he works second shift at Fed Ex.

What was the original intention of the band? Was it meant to be a fun, local party band or was the intent to go all the way and get signed?

Had aspirations of getting signed. That was the number one thing. Being as good as we possibly could to be rock stars. That's what they wanted to do prior to myself or

Ian joining the band. Those guys were driven. And we did it without social media and contacts and stuff. Did we go about it the right way? I don't know if we did or we didn't. There's no formula to success as you know.

Did you produce and demos and pursue professional management?

{Slight hesitation}. *Yes, we did. Did we pursue it as much as we should have, I don't know. We were working with like John Brandt (ex-Cheap Trick), he kinda helped us out in some situations and then when we broke into the Chicago market and met more people. Atlantic Records sent some people out to check us out here in Rockford. With Brandt, he was with Ript, with Steve, there was a couple of songs, "Fair Warning" and "The Harder They Come," Brandt was trying to shop them around a little bit. This was before I came into the band.*

How do you describe Ript's music to someone not entirely familiar with the band?

Our music was a lot of fighting, drinking and fucking. The songs came from the heart and we meant it, true to life depictions of what was happening in our lives at the time. Our fantasies, our good and bad relationships that were happening at that time...

Which leads me to ask about the infamous song "*Spit On It*"

The story behind that, is, a friend of ours named Henry who wound up becoming very big and working for a company called "Power" which supplied power to guys like Michael Jackson and The Rolling Stones when they did shows, and he was friends with Mike Nelson and he was down in Arizona and he met this gal and they were ready to seal the deal and she looked at him and said "If it don't fit, spit on it!" and when you hear something like that you can't let it go, especially Ript, so we wrote the song and it's one of more well-known songs but the groove is real 80's rock and we were opposite of the genre we were in and although we got billed with a lot of those band and might've had the big hair but we were anti "that," we had the premise of "No Poser," you know?

It was all real, no makeup, nothing against that, but, we were all black leather, bad boy, we were a tough band, good fighters. If you listen to our songs, we were a blue collar, working class kind of people that catered to our fans, the Ripsters, who were as important to Ript as the band was to Ript. Without them we wouldn't have had success. We would feed off them, they would feed off us. It was more of a big rock thing where everyone was up at the stage just jamming,

it would create this kind of crazy electricity in the air. At a couple of points in the shows, I'd turn to Utley and ask him, "Are people coming to see Ript or are they coming for the festivities," because there was probably some kind of altercation that happened.

Some of the Rockford bands at the time were Sarkoma, forchristsake…

And we were 180 degrees from any of that. Actually Atlantic Records wanted us to go into a different realm 'cause you had hair bands going out which we were kinda classified in. Prior to myself getting in the band Ript were more of a Metallica, *had more of a British metal kind of thing going on. And before I joined I was more a Flock of Seagulls guy, a European techno pop guy when I got in Ript. I was a keyboard guy with a Flock of Seagulls haircut and baggy pants. But I went over and jammed with Greg and Mike and at that time me and Mike lived in the same apartment complex so we have history together from way back.*

Why do you think a lot of bands out of Rockford came so close to getting signed but didn't make it?

I don't think it was bad timing and the proximity to Chicago was a benefit not a detriment. I don't know, I can't put my finger on it. The Pimps, *later on, did their thing in the late 90's and they were pretty much the offshoot of* Sarkoma *and again that goes back to the formula for success and nobody has that formula.* Hedder, *former* Aunt Flossy, *they did big things. Rockford has always been a music mecca, we're big, there's always been a huge music scene here.*
Even back then there was always a nice competition, everybody supported everybody, there wasn't any real rivalries, per se. But eventually the market got saturated.

But back then, you had a whole scene, you had Minneapolis, Milwaukee, Madison, Detroit, you know, all these cities within like a 200-mile radius of one another.

Was there ever any discussion in the band moving to LA and trying to get signed there?

I don't know. There were some family dynamics going on. In fact, I didn't tour with Ript because I was in the middle of taking custody of my son and that was something that needed to be done at the time.

Nelson was going through a divorce, I was going through a divorce, relationships never lasted in Ript. It was mayhem. Ript was bigger than all of us, it took on its own thing. It might've been the same dynamic that caused the band to implode.

Are you still playing music?

Oh yeah, yeah, all the time. Actually right now I have a trio with my son and a gal named Leanne; it's a very unique, outside the box kind of thing. I play acoustic guitar, bass, mandolin, keyboard, run sound, my son sings, Leanne Leonard plays bass and sings. We have a digital board that sits off to the side, kind of a high tech kind of thing. I've got bass pedals and synthesizers I run off my iPad. We won a Rami for best new act this year. It's a Vegas act, extreme talent, extreme rehearsed.

What about today's music scene compared to how it was back in the 80's / 90's?

I don't know, I think it's kind of neat. Leanne and I go out and support the scene. There's a lot of camaraderie. It's not as fresh and new. Back when we were doing it you had Essie Ecks, Right Mind, Mirrored Image, *forchristsake, and everyone was successful in their own right. I really have to give kudos to Bruce Hammond for the Endless Night thing, bringing in* Extreme, Mother Love Bone, D'Molls *and* Warrant. *I mean, seeing* Extreme *on a Wednesday night with 30 people in the audience and then me and Nelson meeting Nuno Bettencourt, amazing!*

Steve Moriarity
RIPT

What were you doing prior to RIPT and how did the RIPT gig happen?

Steve Moriarity: Prior to ript I was jamming with about three different bands.

What was the original intention of the band as you remember it? Was it meant to be a fun, local party band or was the intent to go all the way and get signed?

Well we wanted to go all the way. We were in the studio recording songs before we even had a set of songs down.

Do you think RIPT could've secured a record deal while you were in the band?

I'll put it this way. When I was in the band we blew away every single band we ever played with. It didn't matter if they opened for us or we opened for them. I won't mention any names but we just annihilated every band.
Fuck it I will mention one. Bad Boy *out of Milwaukee. We opened for them at the* Firecracker Lounge, *Beloit Wisconsin. All the lipstick and blue eye shadow in the world could not help their singer* Xeno *or the band. They were simply out matched.*
We came on like a fuckin' hurricane. They didn't have a chance and that's the way it was every single time we played with another band.
There was no way I would ever let another band get us, even if I had to slaughter the whole fuckin' audience.

Was there any label interest in the band? Were you guys looking for professional management, maybe sending out demo tapes, etc?

Yes, we were. We had an attorney that was managing us. We also had john Brant from Cheap Trick *helping us with some demos and things.*

Was there ever any discussion in the band moving to LA and trying to get signed there?

We talked about it a lot but we were usually drunk. They gave us free drinks every bar we played ya know. So we drank 'em up man I'm telling ya.

Leaving the band, was it amicable?

No it wasn't I ended up playing about ten more gigs after I quit. But I had enough. I just wanted out I had a feeling metal was on its way out. I didn't care much for the new original songs. The drummer was writing songs I didn't think we're metal and I hated singing them.
"Love buckets" was one original. It just wasn't metal. I believe when Ringo Nelson and I were writing the tunes we

were banging. "Hard attack," "See What I mean," "Fair Warning," "Get Ript." *These were the tunes that got us known.*

What's your relationship with other RIPT members today?

I talk to Mike now and then. And I saw Wally the other day at a red light. We talked for a minute.

Have you been asked to be part of any reunion shows?

Yeah Mike asked me to come up and sing a couple songs at their 30-year reunion gig coming up soon. I said I would. It has to be a smashing tune. I can't be singing that pussy shit.

In your opinion did Rockford ever have a shot at getting its local hard rock / metal scene recognized nationally?

Well there were some good metal bands around. The problem was they didn't stay together very long. So I will say, yes there were a few.

Looking back, what would you do different regarding your musical career, with RIPT or not?

Yeah I think I would have still played with those guys. We should have left Rockford early on. But oh well.

What's the local Rockford hard rock / metal scene like now? Is it as good or not as good as it was back in the 80's / 90's?

It's fucking horrible around Rockford. Everybody loves everyone. All these bands are hugging each other, posting stupid pictures online, playing loves songs in a bar. Who in the hell wants to hear love songs in a bar? I want to hear some rock, man, not some tribute band with girdles and wigs on.

Back in the RIPT days all the bands hated each other, tearing down flyers, you know competition. Now boring bands quit at 1am with controlled music volume in the bars by some asshole that works for the bar trying to run sound.

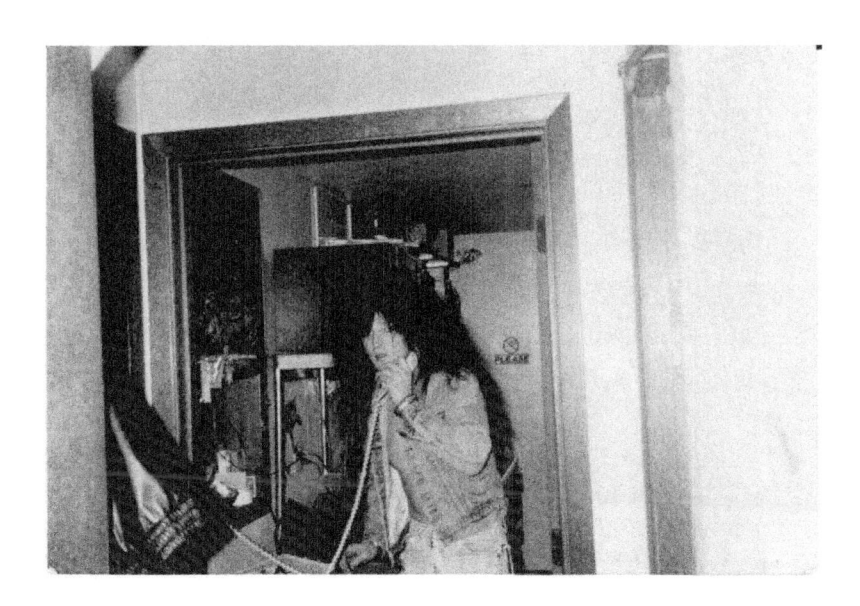

What's your life like today, what are you doing post your RIPT days?

I sing here and there with friends. Motorcycles are my Passion besides music. Harleys only.

Mike Korn
Writer RAM Magazine
Editor Wormwood Chronicles

Mike Korn, Randy Kastner and John Vom at **Days of the Doomed IV.**

  I haven't known Mike long, maybe since October of 2014 when he graciously invited me to write for his website "*Wormwood Chronicles*." It was my return to rock journalism. Prior to that I'd been doing B grade horror movie reviews for "Horrornews.net." From 1989 to 1999 I'd been doing my own zine and freelance writing for others as well.
  When heavy music, namely death metal and thrash, started sounding generic and unimaginative I took a break from it, I got burned out. I did a poetry / lit zine with my father from 2002 till his death in 2010. And then I took another unexpected break because, quite frankly, I was sad and depressed.
  And then in 2013 I responded to an ad I saw on Facebook from Horrornews.net and began writing for them beginning the next week. Mike had been doing Wormwood

Chronicles for a while and I was really into his website; it was a treasure trove of great interviews and record reviews and concert reviews, etc. After six months of writing movie reviews for flicks that never should've been made I left Horrornews.net.

After commenting a bunch of times to music related subjects he was posting on his Facebook page he reached out to see if I'd be interested in writing for him. Of course I was. I was ready to return to rock writing again and it's been my daily obsession since.

Mike Korn is a walking encyclopedia when it comes to metal, he's a true fan in every sense of the word and most of all, he's a genuine, down to Earth guy with a good heart. When I found out he used to write for RAM Magazine, I had to talk him, get his story down on paper.

RAM was the most highly respected music magazine Rockford ever had or will have. Gary Wilmer, RAM Magazine's editor, is still held in the highest of regards. And Mike wrote for his publication, which says a lot about Mr. Korn, himself, as a writer. Invitations like that get handed out very selectively. He got it. He did it.

What year did you start writing for RAM Magazine and what year did you stop?

Mike Korn: *I started in 1995 when a very good friend who was also writing for them suggested I give it a try. My last article for them was either very late 1997 or early 1998.*

Why did you stop writing for RAM?

By that time, the publication had really shrunk drastically and the writing was on the wall. It was a nice thick pub with a lot of pages for many years but had dwindled to like 8 or 10 sheets by late 97.

Plus, I wanted to do something a bit edgier and not as constrained. I don't react awfully well to having my stuff edited, haha!

Mike Korn and Joey Belladona / Anthrax, 2004

How did this rather prestigious local writing gig happen?

It was suggested to me by my friend Denyse Bayer, who thought I might be good at it. She was hugely into the Rockford music scene of the time and actually knew far more about it than I did.
I introduced myself to the editor at that time and things went from there. I did the musical stuff using my own name and I did a column on cult film called "Doc's Dungeon" using my "Dr. Abner Mality" name. That was the first time that name ever got used.

Which local bands did you interview and how active were you in that hard rock / metal scene as both fan and writer?

I interviewed The Six Million Dollar Band, *who later went on to be* The Pimps. *They were one of many Rockford bands who "almost" made it. I also talked to* Throne, Vigilance, Bill, Man Made Man, Kamikaze Butterfly, Submission, *probably some more that my brain can no longer recall.*
I have to say I was a late comer to the local scene. Until the very early 90's, I only casually followed it.... I knew the big names like Cheater *and* Ript *and* Sixx Lixx Fixx. *When I started writing for RAM, I became a lot more intensely involved in it. I feel kinda bad because I missed a lot of great bands from the 80's, when things were really booming.*

Did you see / hang out with Gary outside of RAM Magazine? Tell me about your interactions with him and what kind of guy he was. He was super dedicated to local music, right?

It's a huge tragedy that I never interacted personally with Gary. By the time I started with RAM, he was already gone. I never heard anything but good things about him. His dedication to the local scene was beyond question.
The fact that there's no equivalent to RAM now is something that probably would have really disturbed him but in this electronic jungle we live in today, many publications have been lost.

When you look back at that 80's / 90's hard rock / metal scene in Rockford, how do you remember it now? Was it dynamic, well supported by the fans or the opposite?

I think it was pretty dynamic, especially compared to now. There were more venues that could support live music. I know in the 80's, local rock and metal bands could draw good crowds that could be in the hundreds. Today, drawing more than 30 people seems to be a huge success.
I remember places like Hard Times, Luigi's, Flight of the Phoenix, Prairie Moon, etc. The local record stores were also magnets and generators for the scene.

Looking at today's local music scene versus that 80's / 90's hard rock / metal scene we've been talking about, which one is / was more exciting? How would you characterize today's local scene?

I think lack of diversity has slammed the modern music scene hard. True punk rock is virtually non-existent unless it's in the basement of some squat. I always thought

Rockford was a perfect breeding ground for punk and metal, but somehow it never really took off the way it should have. There are some good metal bands around now, but they seem to resemble each other way too much.

Rockford could use a good thrash metal band, a doom metal band, a traditional Priest/Maiden style band, a black metal band. If any of those are around now, I don't know about them. But metal is not gone, it's still around, it just needs to expand its horizons more and take a few more chances.

Who were the local bands back in the 80's / 90's that you were into, that stand out in your mind?

Going even back to the late 70's, Cheater *and* Red Bud Thunder *stood out a lot.* RIPT *was a super entertaining live band that lasted a long time. In the 90's,* Throne *and* Vigilance *were great bands that knew how to play real metal. In more of the rock vein,* Right Mind *and the* Box Elders *were good stuff.*

There was a really cool prog rock type of band called Ichabod Crane *that played extremely challenging music that I liked a lot.* The Heavils *should have been huge. I keep thinking of more....* forchristsake, Mirrored Image, Xanax, Sarkoma, Egan's Rats. *Many more I'm sure I could think of...*

There were several local bands on the verge of getting signed / garnering national attention. Did you ever wonder if Rockford could be the "...next big scene," maybe the next big sunset strip?

I was hoping that might happen but it never did. There were a lot of bands that were on the threshold and then just seemed to give up. I could never figure it out. Most bands

161

doing original music want to get heard by the most people possible.

There were bands like The Hillworms, Cheater, Fluid Oz and The Pimps that had the momentum...and then it was just like they decided, nah, better not go there. Success can test a band more than adversity. I was really hoping we would get another Cheap Trick. If that had happened, things could have been way different around here.

From your perspective as a writer involved in the local music scene, do you remember what year or what the moment in time was when the local hard rock / metal scene began to lose steam and decline, when the momentum began to shift elsewhere?

There were lots of little declines that added up. When the radio station Y95 was active, they were hugely instrumental in pushing some local bands. When they shut down, it hurt.

In the early 90's, tons of well-known venues closed.... Waverly Beach, Sgt. Pepper's, Great Illinois Purchase, etc, etc. The closing of Appletree and Coop Records hurt a lot. We never really recovered from that.

15 Minutes Record Store and Spin Records tried to bridge the gap but couldn't.... the steam was going out of everything. But I think the end of the 20th Century itself really hurt things. Ever since the year 2000, everything has been a shadow of what it was before. That was the big marker for me.

Was writing for RAM Magazine the impetus behind you starting Wormwood Chronicles?

It got the ball rolling as far as me thinking of writing. As stated before, it was really Denyse who encouraged me to write.

Prior to writing for RAM, did you have aspirations of writing professionally? If so did you go to college and pursue this?

I always puttered around with writing going back to my grade school days. Back then I came up with my own personal comic book universe.

Everybody thought I would be a great writer, particularly my Dad, but I don't have the discipline and patience to do fiction. I majored in psychology in college so a lot of my course load was oriented towards that.

With Mike Korn, Randy Kastner, Renato Brujo and Brian Jugle.

What got you into writing about music, was it the RAM gig?

Even before Denyse talked to me about RAM, I was always doing my own reviews of records I bought. Nobody ever saw the reviews but me. I was greatly inspired by a British heavy metal magazine called Metal Forces. The way I write about music is very much influenced by that magazine. The whole underground fanzine scene of the 80's was fantastic; I'm glad I was around in those days to experience it.

Last question: Tell us about Wormwood Chronicles and where we can find it.

Wormwood is an outgrowth of all my personal interests. Heavy metal is a huge and dominating part of it, but it's not restricted to metal alone. We have quite a few progressive rock and punk rock reviews in there. I like to keep it eclectic but edgy. I still have articles about underground movies, too, although not as much as I'd like.

We also have some regular pieces on paranormal or fantastic subjects. I'm a big pro wrestling fan so that finds its way in there, too. The content has changed since its early days as a paper magazine. You can now find WC at: www.wormwoodchronicles.net. We have tons of archived reviews and interviews going back more than 15 years!

164

MADISON
&
MILWAUKEE

The summer of 1987 was good. I graduated Rock Valley College in the spring with intent to attend Northern Illinois University in the fall. I was in full ON punk / metal mode. Black Flag, The Dead Kennedys, D.R.I., Anthrax, Metal Church, Venom and Overkill were in constant rotation on my stereo. Slayer also.

I used to go to this record store in DeKalb Illinois, half an hour away from where I lived to visit this joint called *"Record Revolution"* to buy punk & metal vinyl, new and used, and get the latest issue of Maximum Rock N Roll or whatever zines they had lying around for free. I loved stores like that. Band friendly. Flyers everywhere. It was incredible. One of my favorite record stores of all time. It was my internet, that's how I got my punk and underground info.

But all of a sudden the world took a serious turn for the awesome. I got turned onto a community radio station out of Madison, Wisconsin via my uncle. WORT. Holy shit, Jesus Christ! I found my version of heaven. Friday night had a punk / alternative show from 11pm till 1 or 2am. It featured local and national acts. It was unbelievable. I'd hear cuts from Appliances S.F.B, Old Skull, Killdozer, Black Flag, M.D.C., the Dead Kennedys, Throbbing Gristle, etc. It was all good until the signal faded on my crappy boombox stereo I had…

I hadn't heard anything like this on the airwaves before. And Madison was already a playground for me. I'd walk up and down State Street buying vinyl at Penny Lane Records and hitting all the great bookstores and game shops along the way. Maybe even a head shop or two.

Madison was a whole other experience when it came to punk **and** indie **and** local band subculture. The city had a built-in appreciation and infrastructure to support the arts, specifically music, local or not. Music seemed like it was the lifeblood of the town, depending what side you were on.

Every light pole downtown was plastered with gig flyers for upcoming shows in the area, throughout the university commons up to the capital. Madison had a distinct vibe, energy whether you were hitting head shops, record stores or venues. The pulse was strong.

The clubs in that town were fantastic. I'd travel to Madison every few months and hang with my uncle going to Club DeWash and O'Cayz Corral, especially O'Cayz where I saw probably 30 bands or so, maybe more. Killdozer, Imminent Attack and The Gomers were regulars on the mad city club circuit. We'd buy records during the day and stash our load and bar hop later. Never, *ever* had a bad time. **EVER**.

WORT had a killer metal show on Sunday nights. That was my "www.pollstar.com." I'd listen to the punk show on Friday to find out which punk / alt acts were coming to town and tune in Sunday nights to get the low down on the metal shows coming to Madison AND Milwaukee. That's how I came to know about the infamous Eagles Club in Milwaukee.

167

What a venue! Every metal band, big and small, played the Eagles Club and that was during the heyday of metal. But it wasn't WORT that clued me in about this place initially. They kinda hammered it home for me. It was a regular, family trip from Belvidere to Milwaukee in 1985, driving by said venue on the very night that the *"Combat Tour"* was taking place with *Venom, Slayer* and *Exodus*. I nearly jumped out of the backseat of the car when we passed by, being a huge *Venom* fan as I was. That feeling of excitement and adrenaline never left me nor did the image of the Eagles Club. It was all burned into my DNA. Forever

After that I saw the name pop up on tour posters for various bands ranging from Celtic Frost (*"To Mega Therion"* tour) to Lizzy Borden (*"Murderous Metal Road Show"* tour). That told me something interesting and exciting was happening there and I wanted to be a part of it. Check that, I **needed** to be a part of it. And the Milwaukee Metalfest, staged for the first time that summer of '87, was my introduction to it.

King Diamond headlined the fest. Nuclear Assault and Zoetrope performed. I was blown away. Life changed at that moment for me. And if that wasn't amazing, a month later I'd see The Mentors and Saint Vitus perform at O'Cayz Corral in Madison.

Saint Vitus changed the way that I looked at and listened to music from that point on. Their live show was near perfection. Their records were equally as good. I remember spending quite a bit of textbook money that I had saved up for school on merch and records. When school started I found ways to get by. It was worth it. My adventures into this world of indie / underground music was just beginning. I was letting go of my small town mentality and discovering bigger and better things that the world had to offer.

Milwaukee, by the way, was a hotbed for metal back in the 80's and 90's. Bands like Acrophet, Viogression, Morta Skuld and Realm were local bands making big noise nationwide and venues like TAverns, The Globe, The

Unicorn, The Crystal Palace and The Odd Rock Café were the venues to see them at as well as other punk / metal acts.

Coincidentally, Jack Koshick, the primary booker at The Eagle's Club and the mastermind behind Metalfest was also the owner of The Odd Rock Café which gained notoriety when GG Allin famously took a dump on stage and then got busted by Milwaukee's worst as well as the site of the Social Distortion riot which made local and national headlines also.

After all these years I found Jack on Facebook. I hit him up for an interview figuring I had nothing to lose and maybe he'd say OK. To my shock he graciously agreed and didn't hold anything back. He answered every question but the thing about Jack, is, he's a down to Earth guy and loves to

169

talk music and has rock N roll stories that movies should be made about, they're that good, that engaging.

The depth and volume of information he provided was mind boggling and interesting on so many different levels it's hard to fully relate my experience to you the reader. This man has lived a lifetime in entertainment and two lifetimes in rock N roll.

But that's Madison and Milwaukee, man. The 80's and 90's were a goldmine of music to be mined by the faithful. It was a great time full of great bands and clubs and outlaw radio.

Courtesy Bob Wasserman

170

Brad Skaife
Imminent Attack

Imminent Attack became of this Earth in 1981, calling both Mount Horeb and Madison its home. The core lineup consisted of Kevin Gayton (vocals), David Gayton (guitar), Brad Skaife (drums), and Mike Hunsberger (on bass). Hunsberger was replaced by Jim Kading and Skaife was replaced by Frank Attway.

Punk was the common denominator that kept them together eventually doing gigs with heavyweight bands like D.R.I, The Dead Kennedys, Black Flag, Motorhead, Exciter, The Circle Jerks, etc. As the band's bio states on their website, "Most of the recordings were done by the guy's over at Smart Studios. Butch Vig and Steve Marker of Garbage if you didn't know." Eventually the band split in 1986 because of lack of money, label, etc.

My recollection of Imminent Attack was going to Madison to buy records on State Street. Madison's punk scene was in full effect. There used to be a small park right off State where a lot of local punks gathered, hung out. I dug that. They were different, they embraced it. To me that was power, or rather, taking the power back from the jocks and meat heads in high school who policed and enforced "normalcy" on the student body.

These guys were the opposite of that. That was very, very appealing to me. This was also the era of the 80's when punk and metal were "crossing over." I was really into Slayer, D.R.I, Verbal Abuse, Dr. Know and Impulse Manslaughter. So this scene was right inside my wheelhouse.

And that's how I found Imminent Attack. Henry Rollins formed a solo band post the breakup of Black Flag and he had a show booked at Turner Hall in Madison. Imminent Attack was the opening band. This was the show I was looking for. Rollins, Black Flag, punk rock, and a band that called themselves Imminent Attack.

I wanted to get in the mix. I identified with punk as much as I did with metal and I wanted to see what Madison's punk community was like. Needless to say my expectations were met. The show was amazing. Rollins was in top form and Imminent Attack destroyed the place. Loud, ferocious, angry rock.

The crowd was great. They really took care of each other from what I remember. I left feeling like I had another community I could hang with. That stayed with me.

Years later I finally got their music and when I decided to write this book the first band I thought of was IA. I tracked the band via their website / Facebook page and spoke with original drummer Brad Skaife who was with the band from beginning to end. This is Imminent Attack, punk rock and the Madison scene in his own words.

Original drummer **Brad Skaife**: *"It all started in our little town of Mt. Horeb. A friend that lived there moved from Maine and brought a lot of musical influences down from there. He also moved to California and was roommates with Duane Peters and skated for Dogtown, Tracker and UFO.*

The first shows were bands that played once and a band called "Genie," Mike and Dan. Never heard of them? How about Killdozer? *That's them. The first band I played in was* BLOODY MATTRESSES *with Jim (bass for IA) Robin Davies (bass for* Tar Babies*) and Bucky (guitar for* Tar Babies*). We played shows from March through Sept then Jim and I left to do the* Imminent Attack *gig and Robin and Bucky started the* Tar Babies.

Mattresses played some epic shows. Black Flag, *when Henry had just joined, and was doing sound check only,* Minor Threat *(one of three shows they played outside DC that year),* Husker Du, *etc.*

The part nobody saw with the Madison scene is we played anywhere, anytime and that usually was a one time as somebody always fucked shit up. I left in 1986 after the Bad Brains *show in Chicago when we were promised $300 and got $100 and it was sold out."*

I was either lucky or dumb enough to keep a journal of a lot of our shows including the west coast tour in 1986. Everything was moving so fast back then. The trasititions in style and influence. Bands today have no idea. They just record and piece it together accordingly."

Here is an excerpt from Skaife's journal of two Circle Jerks shows in late 1985:

Dec 6th 1985

"Imminent Attack, D.R.I, *and* The Circle Jerks *Metro Chicago IL When we arrived I realized a cymbal stand was broken and found a hardware store to get some stuff to fix it.*

Next my drum stool broke and I found a guy that welded it for me. David's new speaker broke and DRI *let him use theirs. (I guess they owed us one as a few years before at a basement party in Madison they used all of our equipment.*

We sound checked and went to our dressing room. The Metro is huge. Sean the promoter who always seemed to be too cool for anyone told us what time to go on. A mixed crowd tonight. Last time we played here we got a really good response. Unfortunately, tonight things were different. The crowd was yelling "go home" and "DRI", blah, blah, blah. I wish I had a microphone as I was feeding into all the negativity. It wasn't all bad as we played good and that is more important than what other people think.

Next DRI *played.* DRI *played fast and tight. They were definitely the crowd's choice. They sure had changed from the 26 song EP they gave me a few years before. Before each band played they made special announcements -- "no stage dives."*

When the Circle Jerks *took the stage the long hairs moved back and the short hairs moved to the front. I noticed a few cans and glasses being thrown from the back of the crowd.*

The bouncers were on edge and definitely wanting some action. They smiled as they pulled people out of the crowd to the back stairs for their final confrontation. They loved beating on people. It might not have been my place but I had seen enough abuse for one night. I blocked the doorway as two bouncers were taking a girl out to the back stage and all hell broke loose.

One bouncer grabbed me by the throat and had me against the wall and was choking me. I swear his eyes were glowing and he wasn't letting up. I believe he would've killed me if it wasn't for the Circle Jerks *singer Keith Morris and their roadie Tony. Sean grabbed me and told me to "get downstage." I told him to "fuck off."*

I wasn't going to give in to what I had just seen and felt something more was going to happen. It did. The big handed bouncer came up and asked me what I was doing interrupting his job? He told me it was his job to control the crowd and he got paid to do it. I said something to the effect of "bet it makes you cum."

He really must take his job seriously! About the same time another bouncer was who trying to stop someone from getting onstage when someone came out of nowhere and pushed him into the crowd. The bouncer who was so uptight jumped in to rescue his bro. (if you can't beat 'em, join 'em, I guess). The band stopped and the show was over. I wanted to kill that bouncer but went to Kevin and David's Dads instead. My neck and throat hurt so bad it was almost unbearable. Monday night we play in Madison with the Circle Jerks and the Tar Babies."

Greenbay WI, 1982

Regarding the D.R.I. mention from the journal entry Skaife says, "DRI. *came to Madison and no one went to the*

175

show. The next night we played at Amy Gehring's house and they used our stuff and played a set before we played.

She was from SF and knew them, that's how they came to Madison. But at the time no one knew them. They played the Wilmar Center. It holds like 150 people. They had the EP out at the time."

Do you think Madison ever had an opportunity somewhere between '89 and 2000 to become the next big, nationally recognized music scene PRE Seattle?

There was so much happening in Madison that it was wasn't "if" it was a "when" Madison would be the place to be. The scene was very tight and there was always something going on.
    ALL the national touring bands came through Madison, and since it was a "do it yourself" scene we dictated how it happened.

What do you think it would've taken to draw attention to the Madison punk music scene and turn that into the next Seattle back in the mid to late 90's?

If someone from a band would've overdosed and died or killed somebody (or themselves) the media would've been all over it.

How close was Madison do you think, to enjoying that kind of national success?

We never wanted to be successful. We just wanted to play music and hang out.

What eluded the Madison scene of this?

Middle America only wanted us to go away. We were a thorn in their side. We played at parks when families were having Sunday picnics.

We played at Neighbor Centers where old people ate meals every day. We made a difference in a lot of people's futures, both good and bad.

What makes Madison or made Madison (in your opinion) conducive to producing great punk bands and a great alt / punk scene?

Again, Madison, WI. Where the fuck is that? We had the newest Black Flag record or saw 7 Seconds when they came through town, but the only scene was what we created.

We decided what local bands opened for National acts, we decided where and when the shows were, we all worked very close with each other. Sometimes you'd have to sneak friends in to a show.

I remember the night Black Flag played in Madison for the first time. It was when Henry had just joined. The show was on the second floor at a club named Merlyns. Serge (who was of Jewish descent) hated The Bloody Mattresses because a friend spray painted our name in front of his club with a swastika. Needless to say, we almost didn't get on that bill, and we played for free anyways.

The front of the building was brick and all these friends were scaling the wall and Dez was pulling them in through the dressing room window. So many of our friends got in free that night. LOL.

IA played shows with The Dead Kennedys, The Exploited and Motorhead. Kennedy's played Osh Kosh at a newly set up place for bands. 1,000 people showed up. 1984 *"Bedtime for Democracy"* tour. Verbal Abuse another San Francisco band was also on the bill as were several Green Bay bands (that I think didn't play). We brought a van full from Mad Town and tore the place up. It was rad.

The Exploited. Let's see, Frickin' cold winter nite, mohawks from England. OI OI OI! Whatever. Motorhead was great. Lemmy was a great guy. We set up in front of their stuff so Kevin (vocals) had to go behind my drums to go from one side of the stage to the other. They were so fuckin loud. 10,000-watt PA in a gymnasium. Lemmy had in his contract three different types of booze. One before, one during and one after the show!

Can you tell me about those shows, where they were held, how well attended were they?

Exploited was at Merlyns. So-so crowd. Motorhead was at Turner hall, a place where a lot of bigger bands played through the years. i.e. Black Flag, SWA, Tom Trocollis Dog, Minutemen, Seven Seconds to name a few.

Do you have any stories you can share regarding any or all of the above bands?

They were all real nice and supportive of us. Most bands we played with told us to get the fuck out of WI and get noticed. Our guitar player was unbelievable and so ahead of his time.
In our last recording you can hear Pantera riffs six years before they were a band. We were always a day late and a dollar short. Never expected too much but sure had some serious fun.

Tell me about the west coast '86 tour. How did that get organized, were you touring as an opener or headliner, what bands did you do shows with? Coming off that tour, was it a success, did it go well?

IF YOU ARE READING THIS AND SET UP SHOWS: If you lead bands to believe they are playing in your town and haven't even promoted the show or forgot to schedule it, you are taking money straight out of the bands pockets and wasting their time. They could be somewhere else playing to people that really care!

If bands can't play they don't have money to get to the next show. We weren't rock stars with a recording deal or label and more often than not we slept in the van or on some one's floor and ate whatever we could find. In New Orleans we ate sandwich meat without bread.

From my journal dated 1986 –

Iowa City, IA Nov. 7TH, 1986

"We arrived in Iowa City about 6:30 and loaded in at a small bar. Iowa City is a college town and who knows what to expect. Half of this place has a bar and pool tables, the other half has tables, a stage, and a small dance floor. The sound man is a new wave techno idiot. Sorry guy. I am sure he has a few great qualities, but he hasn't revealed any as of yet.

The opening band won't tell us what kind of music they play so we'll have to wait and see. We haven't found a place to stay yet. We played a good set to a very small crowd. We decided ahead of time the crowd size will not determine how well we play. Time to load out and get some sleep.

We found an old hotel across from the club and paid $24.00 for 5 people. The room smelled musty and was decorated with old curtains and the wallpaper was very dated. But for $24.00 we didn't complain. The shower was warm and it was a place to sleep.

Nov 8TH, 1986

Where am I and how did I get here? We drove to Kansas City. The show was supposed to be in Lawrence, KS. After a quick tour of Kansas City we arrived in Lawrence only to find out there wasn't even a show. The promoter dropped the ball.

The contact in Lawrence let us stay at her house. Tomorrow we are supposed to play in Omaha if they can arrange a sound system AND an opening band. We'll hope for the best. Minor details. Dorothy and Toto came from here but we couldn't find a yellow brick road anywhere.

The house we are at is nice and the girl told us we'd better not steal anything from her. We told her we didn't do that kind of stuff. No show in Omaha so we have off until Wed. Last night I found out that William Burroughs lives here.

On the road in Missouri en route to Tennessee:

The central Midwest is stereotypically the same. Flat. I have decided if the rest of the tour is this scenic we will all kill each other. Your home must be where you're happy. We drove past Leavenworth Federal Penn.
   We are hoping to find a place to play in St. Louis as we know someone there that promotes bands. If not the next show is Wed in Memphis with Dr. Know. Re: Call to confirm show in Memphis. Someone spray painted "Trust Jesus" on a bridge we just went under. What kind of Christian would graffiti on a bridge?

Nov 9TH, 1986, Cape Girardeau, MO

   Drove from Lawrence, KS to St. Louis MO and tried to set up a show or find a place to stay for a few days. When offered a place to sleep a few months earlier it sounded great but when we called the guy he acted like we were putting him out. Why offer then? So we drove here (Cape Girardeau) and we will call Memphis tomorrow. Hopefully, the promoter will put us up for a few days. Otherwise it's 5 people in a van full of equipment.
   We got a motel room for $20 in Cape Girardeau. That's not each that was the total cost of the room. There is only one bed so we pulled the mattress off the bed and put it on the floor. I am in my sleeping bag by the heater trying to warm up. The blower for the heater in the van doesn't work so it can get cold in the there.

Nov 10TH 1986

Talked to the promoter in Fayetteville, AR and the show there is happening. Cool. Still can't get a hold of the guy in Memphis but as far as we know it's still on. It's Monday A.M. and we are on our way to Tennessee.

In Memphis. We went to Graceland. We couldn't afford to go inside and do the tour (like we're tourists anyway), but walked around and checked out the private plane and stuff. We had a laughing moment in the plane as we all agreed to get rid of the van and borrow "The King's" airplane for the rest of tour. Would he even miss it?

They have a really nice zoo in Memphis and we spent most of the morning checking that out. I picked up some post cards and plan on mailing them out tomorrow. Talked to a kid that told us all the touring bands go to Graceland. We were no different I guess. We might play an open mic thing tomorrow night. Hope to have a good show Wednesday.

Found the promoter's apartment. This place was built in the 60's and is definitely of the low income architecture. After that we went to the Antenna club. Tomorrow night we will be playing there.

The backstage area has graffiti from a lot of bands. They had videos playing and the new Black Flag song "Drinking and Driving" video was on. It was pretty cool.

Back at the promoters apt: There is garbage and cockroaches everywhere. That made me quick to say "I'll sleep in the van and keep an eye on our stuff."

It doesn't seem to bother anyone else. In fact here is a little story about coming in to the apt. the next morning and seeing David sleeping on the kitchen floor amongst the bags of garbage, snoring, with his mouth open.

I wonder how many roaches he ate and didn't even know it? I had to figure out how to shower and change clothes w/out letting them touch the floor and David's sleeping right in the middle of it all!

Being at home with a fire going in the stove sure seems a lot more appealing. It went good except the guy who set it up was from New York and would call us with stolen sprint cards and we were supposed to communicate with them.

Shows not set up, shows cancelled, shows with not enough money for gas let alone food. We were guaranteed $100 in San Fran, $100 in Phoenix and the next show was in Chicago two weeks later with the Bad brains. Does that seem unfeasible?"

You said "I left in 1986 after the Bad Brains show in Chicago when we were promised $300 and got $100 and it was sold out." So what happened post Imminent Attack, did you continue with another band?

I sold all my stuff and pursued my career in drug abuse. It seems that the "rush from playing music" could ALMOST be duplicated through cocaine. Through the grace of God I have been sober since New Year's Eve 1990. And I am not religious.

And I'm assuming since I'm speaking with you about Imminent Attack at some point you and the guys buried the hatchet, right? How did that come about?

There were some years we didn't talk. They went to San Diego (Jim still lives there in his car), Kevin ran marathons and now has sled dogs. David and I had been talking a lot since the release of the CD and he was so excited he was almost in tears when he called to tell me Kevin agreed to a reunion.

Unfortunately, two weeks later, one of the best guitarists I have ever heard was found dead in his apartment from heart failure. Before that David played in White Knuckle Trip. I did a 22-year career with a local Harley Dealership and am now unemployed. My new drum set is in my bedroom and I play as often as possible.

What are you doing today? Still involved with music?

Some friends want to get together to play some cover shit and it's tough to find the intestinal fortitude to do it.

Biff Blumfumgagnge
The Gomers

The Gomers, late 80's. Photo Credit: John Urban

Please introduce yourself. What instrument do you play in The Gomers?

Biff Blumfumgagnge: *I'm Biff Blumfumgagnge, I play strings & drums. Mostly guitar & violin now.*

Do you think Madison ever had an opportunity somewhere between '94 and 2000 to become the next hip, nationally recognized music scene post- Seattle?

Not really. The scene is great here but the bottom line is, it doesn't pay!

What do you think it would've taken to draw attention to the Madison punk / alt music scene and turn that into the next Seattle back in the mid to late 90's? If not how close was Madison do you think, to enjoying that kind of national success? What eluded Madison of this?

Again, there's a rift between playing for fun, often as a student band, and getting paid. There is support but not monetary.

What makes Madison or made Madison (your opinion) conducive to producing great alt / punk bands and a great alt / punk scene? Especially what we saw back in the 80's. Back in the day. Madison seemed like it had a built in audience / infrastructure regarding local music and even music in general -- promoters, fans, zine writers, radio shows, etc.

Great bunch of music lovers... Great bunch of music makers. Rokker/Maxink, and WORT/WSUM all contribute.

Looking back on the Madison alt music / punk scene of the 80's even 90's, was it as strong and dynamic as you remember it or if not, how do you remember it?

It was strong & dynamic & still is! I love the current cadre of music being made/played here.

What's the music scene in general like today compared to back then? Better, worse...

Funny, it might be a little better... More labels, support, and activity. Possibly more venues as well.

Photo Credit: John Urban

What Madison bands are you recommending these days that we check out?

    <u>Kicksville</u> - *great under-appreciated local band!* Buildings on Buildings, Proud Parents, Disembodied Monks, 4 Aspirin Morning, Handphibians, The Flavor That Kills, The Garza, Sexy Ester, Electric Spanking. Reptile Palace Orchestra. The Theremones. Los Chechos .Optometri. Yid Vicious. El Valiente. Phox. Roboman. Honor Among Thieves. Meghan Rose. Harmonious Wail, Damsel Trash. Anna Vogelzang. Cowboy Winter. Helliphant. Steely Dane. *(I'm in* Reptile Palace, Kicksville & Steely Dane *as well...)*

Tell me about the best clubs to do shows at back in the 80's. Do the clubs of today match that of O'Cayz or Club DeWash? Where did your most memorable shows happen?

Most memorable were at Club De, O'Cayz, and then Wally Gators / the Nar Bar. I think the High Noon matches / exceeds what O'Cayz was doing, and the Club de Wash. Some massive memory moments at Bunky's / Club Underground, as well as the Mifflin Street Block party & the Memorial Union.

What was the ultimate goal of the band? Was it to get signed to a record label and tour be a professional musician or was it just be a weekend party band?

In between... Early on we hoped for some signing, but realized that we were a comedy rock band and just had fun with it. Success for us included WMMM playing us weekly for over a decade, and now the Rockstar Gomeroke thing running for 11 years at HNS. It's been Fab-O.
Are the Gomers the oldest local band in Mad City in terms of being together as a band?

We are next to oldest -- Honor Among Thieves *takes that prize.*

Tell me about Gomeroke and how that evolved.

Todd Hanson, head writer of the Onion, told us about Arlene's Grocery in NYC which had a Ramones live band Karaoke show that just killed.
We did a benefit for a health center in Watertown where we charged people money to sing songs with us, and it worked. It grew naturally out of these two things.
Cathy (HNS) wanted a weekly Karaoke show, and I suggested Gomeroke. The regulars have made it a "thing." We're now known as "Madison's House Band" having literally rocked with thousands of "lead singers"

190

Poster by Gordon Ranney

Any famous people you can talk about that have attended and participated in Gomeroke?

Les Paul & Steve Miller both played with us for Les' Lifetime Award banquet. Freedy Johnston, Jay Moran, Kyle Henderson have all rocked with us onstage. There have been others whose names I don't know... Robert Fripp & Adrian Belew have appeared on a couple of our records.

What final comments do you want to include that I haven't regarding the Gomers or the Madison alt music / punk scene or even the local music scene of the 80's and 90's that I didn't cover?

You know I look back on that scene with great fondness - Poopshovel, Cattleprod, Headpump *(which I was in)* Tar Babies, Booty Fruit, Man Clam Chow, Burning Ernies, *etc - very strong stuff.*

Now I feel the scene is just as strong and perhaps even more vital, with more radio / media support, and a new group of bands and fans. The problem still exists that musicians, especially those in the "alt" scene, don't really get paid here, and have to go elsewhere for that to happen.

Madison attempts to make this right with things like "Make Music Madison" however the heart is in the right place but the real issue of supporting musicians here still isn't happening.

Arts should be supported, and they "kind of" are, but the big bottom line still looms and we (musicians) have to go elsewhere to play & tour & get paid.

It's not that I'm bitter or angry or upset; I still love playing here but have to call it like I see it. It's possible to make a living as a musician here, but you've got to teach and possibly have a day job to actually stay alive on music alone.

Killdozer, Garbage, Appliances-SFB *and the Tar Babies all paved the way for Madison to "get on the map" and of course, Smart Studio helped. Now we have* Phox, The Hussy, Fire Retarded *and bands like that who are not only killing it live but creating a scene very conducive to great things... I've seen shows at Mickey's and at smaller, off the map venues that have been great and reveal a super sense of musical community here.*

If you can link to us, we're at www.thegomers.net *and we do private parties, weddings and celebrations of all kinds with our live band karaoke, Gomeroke.*

Bill Feeny
Appliances SFB

Why didn't Madison get the national recognition it deserved with the scope of bands and music being produced / performed back then?

Bill Feeny: *First of all,* Killdozer *made their mark. I don't think the world considered Madison being anything cool. I agree, we had a ton of talent here.* SFB *was courted by a few labels. I remember a letter from Arista saying "Will they compromise, I think not." It's probably true.*

We followed our own interests and our compromise was that we had to entertain an audience. We got a lot of satisfaction from being who we were and that ensemble was loaded with talent. We never tried to create a "hit" - I don't think any of the Madison underground scene musicians did.

Do you think Madison ever had an opportunity between say, 1989 to 2000, to really become a nationally recognized scene in terms of punk and alt rock or was it just not in the cards?

I think the opportunities were there. Garbage *made it to the big time. I have a persecution complex in that Madison was not taken seriously at that time.* Killdozer *recorded at Smart w/ Butch. He can polish a turd. That's not a dig at* Killdozer. *Butch can make anything sound great. Given talent to work with he goes to town. That is why Nirvana came to him.*

Two summers ago some of us remaining musicians did a couple of gigs as Tardozer-SFB *and had a blast. I especially enjoyed playing the* Killdozer *material as I could wrap my mind around it easily and add something to it. I'm not qualified to judge the SFB part of the set only to say it was a ton of fun.* The Tar Babies *material was a bit of a challenge, pretty hard. I didn't feel like I owned it. Um, don't write that.* Tar babies *are wonderful. Pretty far out there.*

What do you think eluded or deterred it from happening on that grand MTV scale in Madison?

Lack of interest or attention. The talent and stage presence was there.

What makes Madison (in your opinion) conducive to producing great local music? And it's not just alt or punk, Madison has a super diverse music scene, always had.

Part of it is the UW which draws artists (kind of a pun in there) to the system and their offspring have a great environment to meet a diversity of talent and like minds. It is always possible to pull a band together with people who truly love performing and finding astounding players and minds.

Looking back on Madison's music scene of the 80's and / or 90's, was it as strong and dynamic as you remember it?

I have many memories which inform me that there was a great synergy between musicians and audience. Madison is not a huge city and it is easy to form friendships. My favorite shows were probably hot summer nights at O'Cayz or Club de Wash when people would gather outside the club and enjoy each other's' presence, get to make social connections.

Once in a while I'll take a cab and either the driver or I would recognize each other from the "glory years" of the Madison music scene. A "hail fellow, well met" scene.

How do you see the local punk / alt music scene today?

I rarely go out. I'm old. I get tired. I sometimes show up. Most of the new music is alien to me unless I share a stage with the act and get enthralled. When I do go out it is mainly to support my friends and see what they are up to. The new scene is alien to me. Not that it's bad, I just don't have the energy to go out a lot. I'm an old fart.

How would you compare the club scene of the 80's and 90's to today? Is Madison still supportive of punk and alternative music or are venues lacking?

I think the venues exist to support continuing music events. They may be kind of crowded. Booking has to be done way in advance.

I'll give you a few venues and you give me some memories regarding them if you could:

Merlyns – Madison – *Heh heh, I can go on and on. Merlyns existed when we began to hit our stride. The load in was awful taking amps up a fire escape. We opened for some popular acts on tour. My favorite Merlyns show that comes to mind was Sun Ra, we didn't open for them.*

We were going to open for Joy Division, *their 1st American gig, and then Ian Curtis went and killed himself. We were offered to open for* Pere Ubu *but I was to be up in the Quetico that weekend. Oh well. Quetico was great. Ubu would have been a lot of fun.*

Interesting Merlyns memory. I think it was a 3 set 3 bux event. Called back for the encore, it was dead winter, we went down to our underwear. All of us had longies except TL who came out in just his underpants. We played a slow, creepy song called Harold. I looked off the stage. Instead of a mosh pit it was a writhing mass of people crawling over each other. I hope I never forget that image.

Many years later the Reptiles *were playing @ Monona Terrace. A family event. We were playing a slow creepy song about a vampire called "The Revenant" by Michael Hurley. I looked off the stage and saw a writhing mass of babies! Crawling slowly upon each other. Parents on the perimeter. It brought me back to that scene in Merlyn's.*

O'Cayz Corral – Madison – *Our home. We had been playing at Rick's Havana Club with acts like* Tar babies, *maybe* Killdozer. *It was tiny. Kay opened O'Cayz up from a country music joint to an anything goes place. O'Cayz and Club de Wash is where I forged a lot of lasting friendships.*
Club de Wash – Madison – Again, our other home. Hot summer nights hanging out in the parking lot. Club de Wash & O'Cayz for a time had a co-op thing going where if you had a stamp from one you could get in for half price at the other if you wanted to see acts at both venues.

Odd Rock Café – Milwaukee – *we played here. I don't have any stories, maybe someone else can fill you in.*

Unicorn Club – Milwaukee – *Not sure if we ever played there. Maybe not. I remember the place so I suppose we did. Waters St?*

The Palms – Milwaukee – *Oh yeah. Once we opened for* John Cale *there. Cale came to the dressing room to introduce himself, said he liked our set but the guitar was too loud. Back to Club de Wash, hanging out after the show, probably with* Killdozer.

A limo pulls up and the window rolls down. It was Cale. He had played at Headliners that night and his driver, for some perverse reason, took him to Club D where he saw what really should have been his audience. I went to his after party at some art studio on Williamson St.

I tried to shoot the shit with him but he wasn't too into it. I had the sense he was just waiting to get to his hotel and had the chore to hang out and socialize with a bunch of musicians, artists and writers from Madison. Another Palms event was SFB, Die Kruezen *and maybe* Couch Flambeau. *Probably other acts, I remember it being some kind of massive event.*

Who were your favorite punk bands from Madison and Milwaukee to do shows with? Any fond gig memories you could share?

Hmm. Hard to say as we were/are all friends. Killdozer & Tar babies *are the acts we mostly played with. There are a ton of others. I'll rattle off a few;* Big Big Bite, Mudsharks, Burning Ernies, Jimmy the Go-Go man, Couch Flambeau, Die Kreuzen *it is impossible to evaluate who was* more fun. There are plenty more and don't have time to sort it out in my head. In most cases we musicians enjoyed each other's' company. That was a given.

Now and then I encounter some from the Milwaukee scene and it is wonderful. A few years ago I was in Amsterdam. There is a club part of the "Melkweg" run by Eric from Die Kreuzen *and his wife. It is called "Eat at Jo's."*

It was a gas to drop in on him. I had warned him I'd be in town but his email had been down and it was a surprise visit. He gave us the grand tour. I love that aspect of networking with people you know and trust. Being in SFB offers me a lot of strange things like that.

Fond gigs: Hmmm. There was a strange show at Club de Wash where less than 50 people showed up. Maybe our strongest set ever? TL turned his back and sang to the wall. Starship in Milwaukee: A Halloween gig where people got all dressed up weird. A woman was dancing in front of me wearing nothing but a trash bag. I think we played with the Oil Tasters *that night. The bass player's costume was to cover his face with band aids. I stole that from him for a Halloween party years later.*

Starship: Someone was demanding we play a Doors song. Huh? We are into our set and I hear glass smashing against the wall. That guy got booted and then arrested. We were told he went outside and there was a police car there, unattended, and he tried to steal a shotgun out of it. Turns out there was a SWAT exercise going on and he got nailed. Okay that is not a good memory. Most of my memories are good.

There was a show at Cafe Voltaire where some guy in a messed up state of mind stumbled into a petite woman who rolled him over and beat the crap out of him. He was escorted out of the club. Months later we, on or way back from a Milwaukee gig, made our usual pit stop near Pewaukee. Hartland Wales exit. When we stop there it is not uncommon to see fellow Madison acts also on their way home. Anyway, this guy at the counter asked what band we were. We told him. "Oh shit! I saw you at Voltaire! I was on X and all I remember is being hauled out!" *That was the guy who Cyndi beat the crap out of.*

Did MTV ever come to Madison to check out the alt / punk scene there?

Not that I know of. If so, they ignored us.

Looking back at the career of the Appliances, are you happy with the band's history or is there a part of you that thinks the ASFB should've been bigger, maybe on par with say Black Flag or The Dead Kennedys?

I am happy with the experience. It is a major part of my life. Yeah, I think we should have been there on the same tier as Black Flag & Kennedys. *Jello once wrote to us when some story compared TL to him. He said he heard more Peter Hammill and Peter Murphy. Later we appeared in a list in the liner notes on a* Kennedys *live release of bands to pay attention to.*

APPLIANCES-SFB
&
BIG BLACK

FRIDAY, JULY 11
AT
CAFE VOLTAIRE

200

Did the band undertake any national tours back in the 80's / 90's?

We played 7th Street and some other place in Minneapolis a number of times. We played all over Milwaukee. Same with Chicago. We had a tour to the East coast and most of the gigs fell through as clubs would change bookers and such. Was going to be a 5 gig tour. We ended up headlining at CBGBs on a Friday, I think, and that place in Hoboken on Saturday.

We also played in Iowa City at least once, maybe twice. I think Killdozer *opened for us at Emelias. Next day we were having breakfast at an IHOP type place and saw Tony Brown (a Madison musician / icon) headed to the other IHOP type place. I ran out to say hello, wiped out on those weird orange stones common by sidewalks and broke my wrist.*

What stopped the band from hitting the road and just becoming a road warrior full on touring band? Was that an option that was talked about internally?

We were up for it. The whole thing becomes complex and we were not able to do it on our own. Also we may have been lazy. We were on the road most weekends doing Madison, Milwaukee, Chicago, Minneapolis and a few other places. It's not so much like anything stopped us, we did not have someone with money and grand ideas in our court. I think we could have had a blast doing a world tour and am confident we would come off well.

Always curious about this -- who named the band, how did the moniker of "Appliances S.F.B." happen?

I'm not sure who named us "The Appliances." It happened when the band was created to play a private party. It was probably Bill Ylitalo, Seth Markov or maybe Tom Laskin. My guess is Bill Y. After we released a 45 we became

201

aware there were other Appliances. One in LA and one in England. For about 6 months we were "Appliances of the North" then TL suggested Appliances SFB. That was a stroke of genius as now we can be found by internet searches if you add the SFB part. Otherwise you get ads from places like Menards. I pity the Residents.

TENSE EXPERTS

with the OIL TASTERS, APPLIANCES
STARSHIP, 5th & WIS   OCT. 31
HALLOWEEN

Just curious. Is digital music and iTunes a friend or a foe to you? That can't be punk, right?

A friend. Without it we would not reach old amigos or interested people. I know it has completely skewed the industry. With the Reptiles it is not as helpful. With SFB I would like people to have access to our music. Not punk at all. Just a way to share painlessly.

We were never a punk band. We embraced the style but it was more like a little bit of color to add to the template of the something, whatever, music that we evolved. Or maybe we were a true punk band. None of us musically trained or informed.

We were a bedroom act that happened to have a few big guns. Everyone but me. I am happy to be a part of it. Laskin, Siebecker, Ed & Scott, I am so lucky to have played with this ensemble.

2015. What are you up to today, what's happening with the Appliances? I hear some reissues have been done, etc.

SFB (pigs on the cover) has been reissued. Is that our eponymous album? Also a few lost tracks were reissued as 3rd and Long. Both available somewhere online. We have been making an attempt to release Them/Green Door but it gets complicated as people's lives move like rivers. There are tons of unreleased bits. A 24 track recording of a set for the "Beat of the City comp."

A few offers to other comps. Some soundtrack things. Some 4 track stuff with Steve Marker (Garbage). I'd love to get them mixed and release 'em. Musically I am playing with Reptile Palace Orchestra (which I created) and my brother Ed is also part of the band. My real job is as the senior illustrator at the UW Department of Zoology. I do some ad hoc things now and then with musician friends.

Dan Hobson
Killdozer

Why didn't Madison fget the national recognition it deserved with the scope of bands and the music being made back in the day?

Dan Hobson: *Madison had lots of great bands back then; Appliances, Tar Babies, Mecht Mensch. Madison isn't on a coast. You needed to be less geographically isolated. Also, Madison is pretty small.*

Do you think Madison ever had an opportunity somewhere between '89 and 2000 to become the next big, nationally recognized music scene pre-Seattle?

Possibly. It might have had a chance to make the big time. I was just discussing this with a friend and we both agreed that Madison would have been more like Athens, GA than Seattle.

What do you think it would've taken to draw attention to the Madison punk music scene and turn that into the next Seattle back in the mid to late 90's?

We needed a band that could have really been popular to a broader audience, like REM *or* Nirvana. *We didn't have a band like that.*

How close was Madison do you think, to enjoying that kind of national success? What do you think eluded or deterred it from happening on that grand MTV scale in Madison?

Madison may have been close, still we were / are not close to the media centers and didn't have HUSKER DU, The Replacements, Soul Asylum, *and* Prince *all peaking at once.*

What makes Madison or made Madison (in your opinion) conducive to producing great punk bands and a great alt / punk scene?

What made Madison great was this bunch of young people not worried about ever "making it." We just wanted to be obnoxious and to sound badass. The careerists who came after Nirvana wanting to get rich, ruined everything.

KILLDOZER

What was the ultimate goal of the band? Was it to get signed to a record label and tour be a professional musician or was it just be a weekend party band?

     Killdozer *really had no goals aside from making the band members laugh. It was a deadly serious joke that lasted for years. We didn't have real jobs, children, or much responsibility back then. And we enjoyed traveling. We were in college back then, and didn't take our educations too seriously. I took out a student loan to pay for our first record.*

206

At what point did you and your bandmates realize that Killdozer had become a popular, even influential band in the Madison punk / alt music scene? I say that because numerous mad city bands cite you as the godfathers of it all even to this day – especially the Appliances SFB.

I thought that the Appliances were the Godfathers of the scene. They were such an awesome band. The reason we might've had a little more success than other Madison bands is because we were willing to tour. We drove to San Francisco to play for $5 bucks once. Believe it or not, Green Day *was our warm up band. They probably made $2 bucks that show.*

What labels did you record for and how did those deals come about?

We were/ are on Touch and Go *records. Great label.*

Did you tour nationally or overseas and if so, who with?

We hit almost every state. We toured with Scratch Acid, Laughing Hyenas, Pussy Galore, Butthole Surfers, *and a bunch of others whom I forgot. We toured Europe multiple times. We were flown to England to play "American Pie" on TV show also featuring* The Pogues *one weekend. We also toured Australia for a month.*

What happened that Killdozer didn't become the next Nirvanna or vice versa?

The reason we never became big like Nirvana, *is because our music was too extreme and uncommercial.*

Did you see events leading up to the end or hiatus of the band?

As far as the band's end, I had a kid, and so I had to stop. They picked up Erik from Die Kreuzen, *another killer band from the era to take my place. That was a good choice, because Erik is so good.* Killdozer *played a few more years with this new lineup.*

Looking back on the Madison alt music / punk scene of the 80's even 90's, was it as strong and dynamic as you remember it or if not, how do you remember it?

Looking back, it really was an exciting time. It was so exciting to always have a great band to see at O'cayz *or the* Wilmar Center. *We fed off of the energy.*

What Madison bands are you recommending these days that we check out?

208

Locally I love The Hussy. *Also* Cowboy Winter *is great. The music lives on.*

Is the band still together or releasing records today?

We haven't played a show since 2011. We might play again for the right price.

KILLDOZER

What's the story of Killdozer today? What are the individual band members doing now?

We all have day jobs now. I'm an RN. Michael is a tax lawyer, and Bill is a grip in Hollywood.

In hindsight, would you do it all over again, the same way?

No regrets at all. I'd do it all again the same way. Punk rock has been the most important thing I've done. I encourage young bands to jump in and do it. Life is too short to not try some hare brained scheme, like playing in an obnoxious, unlistenable band, like Killdozer for a few years.

I KILL YR IDOLS

KILLDOZER
FOR LADIES ONLY
Touch And Go

ON last year's "Little Baby Buntin" album, Wisconsin's Killdozer mauled through the American Dream with their tales of ordinary madness and insanity: women gutted and tied to trees, motorcycle gangs who kill a man by severing his penis and leave it in his mouth, people who throw their mothers downstairs because they think their house is about to burst into flames. Killdozer took gruesome potshots at their homeland, not caring what they hit. Exposing the dark side of the Western psyche, the hidden nightmares, the Freddie Kreugers, the serial killers among us, it was a brutal, damning excursion, the sound of a nation throwing up in disgust at its inner self.

Their new limited edition box set, "For Ladies Only", takes their unique worldview one step further, and tears apart the very culture that American dreams are based on . . . its popular music.

"For Ladies Only" comprises five seven-inch multi-coloured singles, a cover version on each side. On the face of it, it couldn't be more straightforward (or fun). Classic songs come in for some tongue-in-cheek deferential treatment from a *mean*, junked-up, punked-up American hardcore band. But if you listen closer. . .that's when the screaming starts.

By changing the emphasis by the smallest of degrees and adding Michael Gerald's demented barbecued-blackened-chicken voice, while playing some *metal* for kicks, American pop music suddenly turns hideously, unnervingly evil. The scabrous lump of pus lurking behind every beauty spot, the grinning jackass covering for lecherous paedophile and Ku Klux Klan fanatic. "Burnin' Love" is a grisly, grossly overweight, torturously, *wonderful* HM thrash. Conway Twitty's "You've Never Been This Far Before" is a distorted Mekons on 16 rpm. Deep Purple's "Hush" is pure "Black Betty", all na-na-na's and a maximum of thrust.

It's on the more famous songs, however, that Killdozer's grotesque vision truly comes into being. Their versions of Don McLean's repugnantly poignant "American Pie" (Parts 1 and 2, natch) and Coven's "One Tin Soldier/The Legend Of Billy Jack" are *total*. Confederate history as it should have been written (by the Indians), bloodied corpses returning unbowed for their final curtain call. Michael's spewed-up dredged-up voice rips the very *essence of being* out of the classics and turns their meaning to an exact opposite while remaining ridiculously faithful to the originals.

There's a line on "American Pie" which chills my blood to ice everytime Michael gets his tortured larynx around it. "Well I know that you're in love with him/Cos I saw you dancing in the gym. . ." If voices could kill. . .this would be tantamount to the first degree!

Lines such as "Go ahead and hate your neighbour/Go ahead and cheat your friend/Do it in the name of Heaven/You will justify it in the end" on "The Legend Of Billy Jack" remind me of Savage Pencil's latter-day truly *demonic* creations, all monster and no head, Lemmy if he ever lost his voice.

Elsewhere, Steve Miller's "Take The Money And Run" sounds a little perfunctory, "Funk #49" is total mayhem overkill, closer to Killdozer's own fare, and Buffalo Springfield's "Mr Soul" is more of the same. Killdozer have totally *decimated* the American dream, with mindwarping glee. How can these (people?) live with themselves?

EVERETT TRUE

Mike Turnis
Horny Genius

Horny Genius wasn't around a long time. What were the years you were active and why not longer?

John McNeill, Brian Hageman and I started this whole mess in 1983 while we lived (and grew up) in a small rural Iowa town (Monticello) We were drawn together by the punk, new wave and (later) hardcore music that was around on college radio in the late '70's and early 1980's. But being in a small town did not give us much a chance to do things that we really wanted until (luckily) we met some people from another small town (Manchester, Iowa) that were living in Iowa City. These folks were John Frentress, Anne Eickelberg, Mark Davies, Gloria Sands and Scott McWilliams.

They were playing in a band in Iowa City called

the Total Fools. *It was through them that we got a chance to do live shows in the Iowa City underground scene. (The Fools would later split up, with Anne, Mark and Brian moving to San Francisco to form the* Thinking Fellers Union Local 282. *Scott McWillams then became our regular drummer as he was splitting time with Horny Genius and the Fools.) I might add we had several other names before we became Horny Genius, among them the* Mental Midgets, the Detractors *and* That Matters *and some rather original other ones we had that got lost in the shuffle,* Hand Grenade Boner Penguin and Buckmenster Fullers Geodesic Missiles.*)*

After Brian left we chose Scott Siegling to take his place. We knew him from another band and after meeting with him for a few pitchers of beer we made that fine decision. Scott lived on his folk's farm in West Branch, just outside of Iowa City and his parents were cool enough to let us use the old chicken coop for a practice space, and later their garage, with a potbelly stove, for our winter practice quarters. Guests were able to sit on the tractor in garage whilst we did our practice thing. Lee Siegling (Scotts' dad) would once in a while come in, throw another log into the stove and sit and listen to the cacophony that enveloped the area.

For those maybe not familiar, what type of music were you guys doing?

We were indie rock back then before it was called that. We had numerous influences as we had quite an eclectic taste. Punk and hardcore being one of them. "Blender music" was what John called it then. Take all of things that we like and blend them up into our own unique stuff.

You were based out of Iowa City, IA but spent some time in Madison's club scene. Why specifically Madison?

MIKE   MUFFIN   SCOTT   JOHN

COMMUNITY 3
438 Bedford Avenue
Brooklyn, N.Y. 11211

HORNY GENIUS

  It was through word of mouth (networking we did back then). Stickdog *and* Stiff Legged Sheep *were Iowa City bands that we became friends with and it was through them playing and recording in Wisconsin that tipped us initially off about Madison.*
  I had visited Madison before as my sister moved there in 1986 to start her nursing career. It was the first time I had been there and it was love at first sight. How can it not be, as beautiful as it is on the lakes and downtown? Later in like 1987 or so John and I went to go visit and explore the scene and were pretty impressed with what was going on. Stuck with us ever since.

214

What year did you record at Smart Studios? And was it Butch Vig that produced it? Tell me about that experience recording there. Now it's kind of an iconic place, what was it like back then?

*Smart was just an old building on East Washington Avenue then. From the outside it did not look like much, maybe an old corner liquor or grocery store at one time? We recorded at Smart in June 1989. We went there because of an Iowa City band (*Stickdog*) recorded there and said good things about working with Butch. We also liked his work with* Killdozer *(who played shows with* Stickdog*) and when we found out he was not too pricey at that time we were sold. Actually Butch was credited as the engineer and the dude who ran the label we were on at the time was the producer.*

I recall when we recorded, we got there on a Sunday and were finished with everything the next Saturday. We were well prepared with our songs since we had playing them live and because of that we got through things quickly. We made a joke about Michael Gerald of Killdozer *singing with us on a song and Butch offered to call him and ask. We were amazed when Butch told us Michael would do it for a beer and be right over!*

Smart was also trying to earn extra money back then and we met Steve Marker on the second floor of the building working on some surveillance tapes for the Madison police dept. I guess it was for a future court case. Steve was busy trying to clean up the background noise so the evidence could be heard more clearly in court. Never did find out if the accused were found guilty or not.

And if you met Butch, tell me about him as well. Was he down to earth, cool guy to work with? Did the band and he ever get together outside the studio for drinks, etc?

Yes he was a very down to earth and cool guy to work with. He was pretty laid back, maybe even like a yuppie or

215

something like that back then. He offered suggestions when the time came for one. He was not pushy. We did not go out for drinks and the fact that but we did bring our own beer (quite a few cases of Huber if I recall) he was ok with that. Killdozer set the precedence for cases of beer I understood.

O'Cayz and Club deWash -- Can you give me your experiences either playing there or hanging out:

O'Cayz – Madison -- *We played there a few times with Poopshovel and Drug Induced Nightmare # 4 and it was fun every time we did. Pretty unique place with the stage by the front window...I recall one time when we were on our way to one show the van broke down near Platteville so we had to pile in my car with only our guitars and had to use Drug Induced Nightmare's amps and drums. Turned out to be great show. Plus there was always the, ah, "extracurricular" activities going on in the back of the place if you know what I mean.... (Ask Poopshovel what I meant.)*

Club deWash – Madison -- *We never played here but we came up to see our friends the Thinking Fellers play there in 1989. Was a great place too, wish we had played there...*

We did play a show with Die Kreuzen *in Milwaukee. It was on a Midwest tour we did for the album* Burn Your Sister*. Show was in 1990. It was at the Unicorn, a place located in an old slaughter house by what was then County Stadium. Manager of the place was a Greek guy who made excellent Mexican food! Crazy thing was after the show we drove to Chicago to stay with a friend there and arrived at his place at about 6 AM.*

216

Who were the bands back then in the Madison music scene you were friends with? I know Poopshovel was one of them. .

Poopshovel were on the same label as us and we met them when John, Scott and I came up in November 1988 to meet with our record guy. Great guys and still great friends. Always a blast to hang out with them. It made it a logical choice when the record guy arranged a European tour later in 1990 that we went over together. I think Bill Crawford ended up by chance meeting Dizzie Gillespie at Schiphol Airport in Amsterdam, had him sign Bill's horn case. We were also friends with Cattleprod *another Madison band on the label we were on. Great to hang out with them too!*

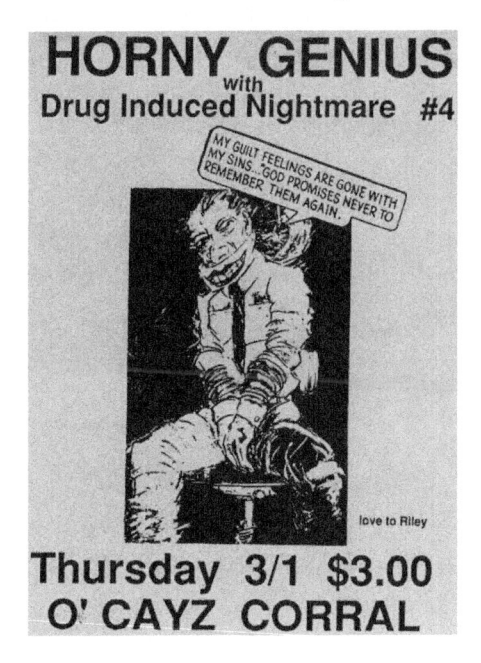

HORNY GENIUS
with
Drug Induced Nightmare #4

MY GUILT FEELINGS ARE GONE WITH MY SINS. GOD PROMISES NEVER TO REMEMBER THEM AGAIN.

love to Riley

Thursday 3/1 $3.00
O' CAYZ CORRAL

Tell me about the Poopshovel tour.

As mentioned previously it was through our record guys' connections. We went over in 1990 and toured the Netherlands and Germany. It was an eye opening experience for me since I had never been to Europe before. Amazing to see East Germany a year after the Berlin Wall fell and get a glimpse of what life was back then for East Germans. It was a great time though and was really my first view of European culture. We made friends with a lot of people in Holland.

Did you see the end of Horny Genius approaching or did it surprise you?

I really don't see it that we ended. Being in this group is kind of like being in the Mafia, once in you are there for life. But we just wanted to do other things in life in 1991-92. I really feel we have been on an extended break since. (ala the Membranes, *a long holiday mate!) We still keep Horny Genius somewhat active by reissuing and issuing music on our own label Pooter Records. We recorded a lot of our shows and our practices so there is a ton of tapes (over 100) that I am slowly going through and (re) issuing what we can. Plus we still have some unreleased studio things to put out, eventually.*

Looking back now, was the alt / punk scene as strong as you remember it in Madison or not so?

Madison was one of the best in the Midwest because of groups like Killdozer, Tar Babies *and the* Appliances SFB *(and of course* Poopshovel *and* Cattle Prod*). I am not too familiar what Madison has now but what I have heard from, the Hussy is pretty good.*

Iowa City's alt / punk scene was pretty thriving too I might add. Bands like Red Throb, Peterbilt, Iowa Beef Experience, Stiff Legged Sheep, Day Glo Bomber Boys, Stickdog, Tape beatles. *All pretty darn good. We had a lot going on for us then and still now really. Iowa City is still going strong with artists like* Wax Cannon, Cone Trauma, Illinois John Fever, Acoustic Guillotine, Ed Gray.

Is the scene today better than it was back then or not? Why?

Then it was more do it yourself. Posters were made a print shops, not on computers. You had to go to a studio and record, or record yourselves on boom boxes. You had to call about getting a show. Now you can pretty much do it all yourself without a studio or put things out without a label or via email and social media.
I think today's bands have it so much easier in that end of it. Mainly through the existence of internet and arrival of digital music and digital video. We sure wish we had all of this technology at our finger tips back then. Connecting with other bands, getting gigs, making videos. That is all so much easier now.

What is life like post Horny Genius?

Good thank you! John and I live in the Madison area now, Scott Siegling is still in the Iowa City area as is Scott McWilliams. Madison is still a great place and when I tell people I live in that area I always get some pretty positive reactions. We are all still are bitten by the music bug and keep active one way or another. John played in a group called Snotwhistle *in the Madison area and has also done some great solo things as* Planet Corral *and* Orphaned Pennies.
I mess around with musical stuff as Wovoka JR. *Mostly having fun recording at home but recording with friends too, like with John or Ed Gray. I played a live solo show once in Holland but found out that was not my cup of tea so I only do recordings and make the occasional video for You Tube. Scott Siegling recorded in a group in Iowa City he formed with Scott McWilliams,* Little One, *which is*

quite good too thank you. After (still) traveling this musical journey over the years (and meeting lots of friends), I would not trade it for anything in the world. It's been great!

Blunt Rapture
Cattle Prod

Why didn't Madison get the national recognition it deserved with the scope of bands and music being produced / performed back then?

Blunt Rapture (bands Cattleprod & Headpump): *Who knows? I moved to Madison FROM Spokane Washington where* THAT *scene was burning. There is a documentary of the Spokane scene at Spokanarchy.com Spokane seemed to have exactly the same problem as Madison—churning out amazing art but no "movers and shakers" would ever hang. So no scouts were ever scouting. They wouldn't travel far enough to check on eastern Washington; no one would go past Milwaukee in search of.*

Do you think Madison ever had an opportunity between say, 1989 to 2000, to really become a nationally recognized scene in terms of punk and alt rock or was it just not in the cards?

Yes. So did Spokane. But Madison was amazing.

What do you think eluded or deterred it from happening on that grand MTV scale in Madison?

Like I said: for some reason, scouts and AR people would not visit.

What makes Madison (in your opinion) conducive to producing great local music? And it's not just alt or punk, Madison has a super diverse music scene, always had.

The seat of the university and capitol, Madison was in the hotbed of all sorts of things. A history of political unrest and student demonstrations, etc., also helped.

Looking back on Madison's music scene of the 80's even 90's, was it as strong and dynamic as you remember it or if not, how do you remember it?

It seemed huge. Cattleprod *was lucky enough to climb very high into the "scene" until we were opening for* Garbage *at the Barrymore. Most bands were very cool and sociable. Some actual art in amongst several jangly-dangly bands. Every band was so helpful! Dave from* Poopshovel *drove home and got me a new cord so the show could go on.*

How do you see the local punk / alt music scene today?

I have moved back to Spokane, so I'm not sure about Madison. BUT it seems, just like landlines and televisions, it may be gone—until the new cage-rattlers have an idea. Cattleprod *was a reaction against musical bullshit — like* Nirvana *and* Pearl Jam *but we were but not so bar rock butch.*

I know most of everybody from Mudhoney *to* Screaming Trees, *etc etc. I opened a club in Spokane in an old garage that showcased bands from* U-men *to* Meat Puppets. *I still have a tape of* Screaming Trees *trying to get a gig by sending me covers of* Led Zeppelin.

How would you compare the club scene of the 80's and 90's to today? Is Madison still supportive of punk and alternative music or are venues lacking?

That's what may have changed here. No one goes out to hear a band anymore, and often go home early. Madison is just on that tipping point of small and cool but becoming bigger and unwieldly. Being within walking distance to several venues really helps Madison stay in the game.

Tell me a little bit about Steve Marker (Garbage) and Cattleprod.

Steve Marker toured with Cattleprod on our "College Hit" tour. He played guitar. Steve liked us from recording and joined us for the tour.

What year was that?

Damn. 1986 or 1987? I would have to search to be absolutely sure what year that tour was

Was he working for smart studios at that time?

Yeah, that's how we met. We sent our cassette in an empty pizza box to Comm3 in New York. He signed us. Comm3 was the guy that first recorded 1000 Maniacs *which is not my cup of pop tea. He wanted to produce a record with us in Madison.*

If you're going to make alt music in Madison, you go to *Smart Studios. Butch Vig and Steve nurtured us along. Oh yeah, also* TAD *showed up to record and I got him weed while he made me a sandwich. People would show up and hang out.* Tar babies *spontaneously played percussion on our first LP. Tad showed up on the second LP. Also* Run Westy Run *and* Sonic Youth *did background vocals. In Spokane, me and a friend opened a garage as a club, "Moe's Bodyshop," and all the Seattle and Ellensburg bands wanted to play. We even had a hole in the ceiling, chicken-wired over. So the skatedorx built a half-pipe over it and they could see down and the crowd could see up.*

Anyway, that was why I knew him. And getting back to TAD *while we were recording,* TAD *was hungry when he got into town, figured I could help him find weed. He went upstairs while I recorded vocals downstairs and made me a sandwich for helping. And Dave Pirner druggedly helped us do some background noise for our second album called "Boost." Smart always had celebrities dropping in, I just had a northwest connection.*

Can you talk a little bit about your time at Club de Wash?

CLUB DE WASH! I bartended and played there. It was a weird home away from home, the kind of club you will never see again. Club de Wash was the buddy bar with O'cayz, in a lot of shit together. Even us bartenders played softball at Georgia O'Keefe on the weekend.

Toni (Zeimer) would wear a holster holding shot glasses and whisky. When we got a base hit or stole, she would jog to the player and do shots. Also each player had a beer bottle next them on field. If you got a hit and were able to grab a beer as you ran by, it was all good. I look back on it now and its like, did we really do this, really see this shit?

Georgia O'Keefe field?

Yeah, over on Madison's near east.

What bands do you remember playing at Club de Wash?

I remember The Burning Ernies *and* The Gomers *always playing O'Cayz and the Club. We had days of oddness: One Sunday you could find a bunch of local bands,* Jonathan Richman (Modern Lovers), Liz Phair, *etc., drunk and playing softball or kickball.*
Smashing Pumpkins, *sure, lots of bands, from* Morphine *to* Pere Ubu *stopped in at the club's green room to get for the show and get green.* Morphine *always came to me for the ganga.*

Just to be clear, geen meaning pot, right?

Yeah. Pere Ubu *but not David Thomas, the singer. He gulped honey from a plastic honey bear jar that his band hid from him on the ceiling heater duct to get him revved up to perform. Since I was a bartender and also lived there, it was just easier to ask me. I wasn't a dealer but I could work things out.*
Ever field any kinky requests?

Kinky requests? There was very interesting activity of all sorts that found its expression in the rooms within the hotel, involving restraints and spankings perhaps.

You lived at the Club de Wash, upstairs?
About 4? or 6 years I lived above the club? I was also across the hall from the gay bar DJ booth and the dressing

225

room, so I learned intimate details about how drag queens prepared for their performances.

Would the club "*accommodate*" if such a "*need*" struck a customer, maybe?*I mean, sure it wasn't a whorehouse per se, but, I'm sure it "accommodated" -- had to be sex, drugs, and rock N roll, that's the thing. Since the hotel was above the club, bands would perform and stay there.... "Stuff" would happen.*
Often the hotel was full of drugged out amorous gay guys that suddenly noticed rock stars were hot. They would "end up" in a band's room. And gawd yes. It was a one stop shopping center -- drugs, drugs, drugs. I would have people knocking on my door at 5 am and offering to do coke with me.

And did you?

Rather not say but I am known for my libertine scofflaw ways. New Year's Eve at the club was insane in a bit of another way than O'Cayz.

I'm almost imagining, with you guys managing and promoting at both O'Cayz and Club D, it seems almost incestual in terms of the bands you were partying with. It had to become weird at some point. Or maybe not?

It was very incestual. Madison isn't a big enough town to have east and west music sides. Sometimes Club D would help O'Cayz, or vice versa. When the floor at OC caved in, Club D stepped up and opened their bar to displaced shows.

Did I mention I was once the beer slave for Dave Atell *and* Lewis Black *at the Barrymore and we ended up at a strip club?*

226

Last thoughts?

From 1984? I'm having a manly misting. I spent so much time there on and off stage, drunkenly tossing everyone's keys in their drinks and getting carried out, avoiding certain areas of the basement, accidentally falling off stage and somehow grabbing wheelchair handles and gymnast-flipping over and into the crowd so as not to crush Rachel, hating and loving a certain manager simultaneously, thrilling to Brian Brecht lighting powdered creamer, the legends and locals, the detachable floor, and snapping towels with the weirdest coolest scene ever.

LOVE YOU O'cayz/Comic Strip and LOVE ALL OF YOU freakwads that were part of it. The weirdest thing was looking at the 6 foot by 6-foot lot left over. WTF? All of that epic shit happened in an area the size of a hotel restroom?

Bucky Pope
Tar Babies

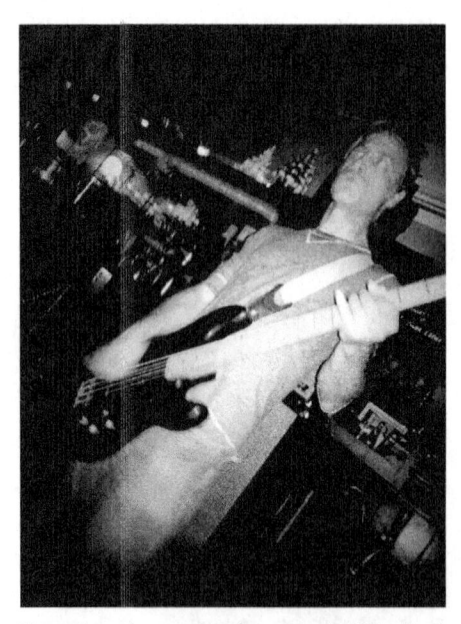

Why didn't Madison get the national recognition it deserved with the scope of bands and the music being made back in the day?

I loved "Nevermind" when it came out. In terms of grunge rock, I wasn't moved too much by a lot of the bands that emerged and began the label frenzy that Steve Albini critiqued really well, which I read on Facebook recently. In 1990 I thought Madison was great because the Tar Babies *drew big crowds. It was great for my ego. I wasn't jealous of Seattle at all.*

In terms of Madison not getting its due? In some cases, sometimes it doesn't seem like the arts community in Madison wants it bad enough, whatever "it" is, being better than just really, really good. Life has always been pretty comfortable here. Maybe there isn't enough tension here to push serious artists / musicians to break out and command attention, if that's what they want. Maybe I should just speak for myself.

All of the above would apply. I can't explain it any better. Madison definitely mattered during the hardcore punk years. From '81 to '85 Minneapolis, Madison, Milwaukee and Chicago all had people who were willing to find alternative venues like churches, parks, parties, mason temples etc. so

228

that punk bands from either coast could gig across the US and know they could play clusters of shows around here. DC, Boston, NY and LA had the most notorious scenes, but weren't on Rolling Stone or MTV's radar, so it hardly mattered to anyone.

Memories of Merlyns and O'Cayz:

I was in high school during Merlyn's existence, so I had to sneak into every show I saw there. The drinking age in Wisconsin was 18 in the early eighties so if we faked a hand stamp or had a fake id we weren't as conspicuous as a 16-year-old might be trying to get in to a club today.

There was also a fire exit at the back of the club that led down a stairwell to a hallway Merlyn's shared with the gyros restaurant next door. We would just have a friend who was already in walk by and pop the door while we waited. If nobody saw us we'd scatter like cockroaches and pretty much blend in.

Between '80 and '82, I saw Bad Brains, X, Iggy Pop *two nights in a row,* The Slits, Black Flag, Selector, Revillos, Fear, Stranglers, the Ventures, *and many more bands that cool rock people who were born too late would die to see.* Sun Ra *played there. I have a few friends who either worked there, or were just there a lot, who could explain Merlyn's better than me.*

I experienced it through the eyes of someone who had to sneak out of the house in order to sneak into Merlyn's. It was all mind blowing to me, even without the music. Merlyn's was like an outpost of cool among the hordes of frat boys and other meat heads who weren't accustomed to seeing dudes in leather jackets making out with each other on State Street, or skate punks with green hair, who would actually hurt them badly if taunted sufficiently (R.I.P Otis).

There were countless numbers of people who weren't ready for Merlyn's cruising State St. at that time, and

Merlyn's presence did provoke some psychic discord with the straights. And maybe for good reason, its liquor license was yanked do to too many police calls. You might say it stabbed itself in the foot (R.I.P Serge). I think the first show I crashed was U2, *but it might have* Ultra Vox. *Who knows it's been thirty-five years. I do know that I missed* The Specials.

One of the things I loved about O'cayz was how haunting the jukebox sounded when no one was in there. Playing "Crazy" by Patsy Cline *or "Papa's got a Brand New Bag" made me feel like I was transported back to 1965. It felt like the ghosts of the ne'er do wells who sat at that bar thirty years before were still there being as stupid and getting as over served as we were, and would have been if the place hadn't eventually burned down. What would the Comic Strip have been like in 1969? The old hags wouldn't have been throwing shot glasses at the other old hags because they would have been checking their phone for updates.*

    I remember being jealous that the Royal Crescent Mob *caved in the floor of O'Cayz. I knew the* Tar Babies *had done 90% of the work on that floor. The* RCM *just happened to be in the right place at the right time.*

Helios Creed *told the crowd that he was glad he wasn't the biggest asshole in the bar while watching me going to great effort to photograph his effects pedals.*

[Flyer: HELP US FEED THIS STARVING GIRL. 4 BANDS!: MILLIONS OF DEAD COPS! (FROM SAN FRANCISCO!) – DIE KREUZEN! (MILWAUKEE!) – TAR BABIES! (MADISON) – KILLDOZER! (MADISON) at Nottingham Co-op (146 Langdon) FRI. APRIL 22, 9 PM only $2.50. HELD CAPTIVE for 10 YEARS IN NOTT. Co-op! OUCH! MY BACK HURTS!]

Current Projects:

My project now is called Negative Example. *We've self-released an album, "Negative Examples." We'll have a three songer out this fall. We're on Bandcamp, so go listen to it. I love it. I have Dave Adler playing keys, an upright bass, drums and another guitar player.*

I'm really proud of my new songs. We're never going to tour and we'll probably not have a video on YouTube. Our Facebook page gets views, but there's nothing to look at. I just want to keep writing and recording and play live every once in a while.

O'CAYZ CORRAL
Honoring a Madison Institution

Wikipedia Description:

Located at 504 E. Wilson Street in Madison, Wisconsin, USA, O'Cayz Corral was originally named Don's Shell (Owned by Don & Cay Millard). Later named, "Millard's Bar." Catherine "Cay" Millard became owner of the tavern in 1980 and changed the name to O'Cayz Corral, a country-western themed bar with a capacity of 150.

It was operated by "Cay" until her death in 1990. Four of the children (Mike, Mary, Pat, Don) formed a corporation "*Cayz Corp*" and ran the business then leased the club to Cathy Dethmers in 1994. Cathy Dethmers, leased the business until 2001.

Referred to as the "*CBGB's of the Midwest*," O'Cayz featured many underground punk, grunge, and rock bands that later became major contributors to pop culture. People best remember two events at O'Cayz, aside from the many fine performances there.

A drunk truck driver smashed into the front of the building, killing a 22-year-old University of Wisconsin student and destroying the band Surgery's van. On another occasion, the floor caved in on the dance floor during a Royal Crescent Mob performance. O'Cayz was destroyed by a fire that began in the 'Cay's Comic-Strip', a neighborhood bar at 502 East Wilson St., also owned by the family of Cay Millard, on January 1, 2001. Dethmers reopened nearby in 2004 as the High Noon Saloon.

233

James White: *"83-87 was my time for standing on the bench on the east wall, always showed up early to get that spot with Mark Poroli and Mike Lally, then sometimes after the shows go climb buildings for a night cap toke, called ourselves urban mountaineers, or sometimes hop on a slow passing train back towards club de wash near where we lived, really good memories, really good shows, really good friends..."*

Source: *Friends of O'Cayz Corral* Facebook Page.

Robert Corbit
Worked at O'Cayz & Club de Wash
Local Musician

You worked at O'Cayz. What years and in what job capacity?

Robert Corbit: *I worked* O'Cayz *for Tom Layton & Kay Mallard from 1985-90's? Started doing the door for him when I was about 17 and also was trying to book my band at the club. Tom would book all kinds of great music at O'Cayz and different clubs around Madison, including Turner hall and whatever Venue would fit the band.*

Tom Layton his company was Lame Brain productions. *Kay was really nice but hardcore business; she was like a gruff grandma. You knew she cared about you. She really trusted Tom.*

I was also doing load-ins and working stage security and change overs with others for these shows. He'd book local bands to be the opener and in some cases do a lot of flyers. There were tons of great bands in Madison.

After Kay died and her daughter Mary took over (who didn't have a clue how to run a club), Tom left and started working with First Artists doing different bigger shows.

I was asked to help manage O'Cayz and was happy to do so, but it wasn't the same club. Tom & Kay made that place awesome. Eventually I left and went on tour with the Tony Brown Band *as a tech and back up drummer for a summer tour.*

Take me back to that time. How old are you and what music are you listening to?

I was raised with a professional musician who toured with national acts and played a lot of Madison clubs and was

235

already known to the Club de Wash and Layton when I went to work in the club scene. Back then the drinking age was 18 and you could work in bars if you had permission. Plus I'd go to a lot of my Dads gigs till midnight on weekends.

I was listening to everything from Funk to reggae to Punk rock and the sub pop stuff. I have been sitting in with my Dads bands since I was 10! So whatever he was playing in, like Clyde Stubblefield or Paul black, and a lot of the other gigging musicians, I knew like uncles.

[Flyer: brutal truth / bongzilla / the NIGHTBREED / SENOR LULULALO — SUNDAY, JULY 26 SHOW AT 5:30PM — ALL AGES $5 — O'CAYZ CORRAL, 504 E. WILSON ST. (608) 256-1348 — RHETORIC RECORDS]

What's it like working with guys who book shows. I'm sure you were there to meet the bands, maybe hang out and party with them. Who / which bands stand out in your mind regarding this?

Tom was always pushing and got along with most bands. You could tell he had everything down systematically in his head. He was always on edge to make guarantees and keep the bands happy. Toni Z from the Club de Wash would step in and help on the bigger shows.

As the opener on some shows they would need to use my set or the opener's gear. The Melvins *needed a drum set and I never heard of them. I watched with my jaw hanging open and in awe when he beat the shit outta my 1964 Slingerlands. I was blown away and pissed off at the same time. I saved a couple heads with dents in them and gave them to a huge fan. They were awesome.*

We hung out with a lot of them, I could fill this page! We played like 3-4 gigs with the Smashing Pumpkins *while they were recording their Album at Smart Studios. I had them play a benefit I put together for $100 and an after bar party. They stayed at my then girlfriend's house. About a week later their huge CD was released. Jimmy still hung out but then they took off!*

The Dwarves, Kyuss, Soundgarden *all played there to little crowds, right before they went worldwide. Opened for* TAD *3 times;* Skinyard *that had producer Jack Endino in it. The club's dressing room was in the basement which was dark and dank and had water whenever it rained so they didn't hang out much down there. I spent 8 years there so there are a lot of cool band stories.*

What was the attraction that O'Cayz had with local Madison music enthusiasts, fans and bands alike?

It was just a cool dive bar vibe. Almost everybody in there was a musician or just loved music. Next door was the Comic strip that had a killer 40's and 50's dive bar feel with some way out, older career alkies -- and Kay owned both of them.

All the Rockers hung out and there was music almost every night. You would always read about a band coming there because Tom booked some great acts and always had local bands open and he made sure to support local music. Tom knew it would create a great scene. The Club owners worked with each other too, to not book against each other.

[Mike Watt poster — WITH TRANSFORMER LOOTBAG • SEPTEMBER 27 • O'CAYZ CORRAL]

What were some of the shows that still stand out in your mind as being the best you saw at O'Cayz?

Brother!! 24-7 Spyz *and* Primus, Living Color *and* Primus, Killdozer, Soundgarden, Big Jack Johnson, The Oilman, Bitch Magnet, The Jesus Lizard, Tar Babies, Helmet, Royal Crecesnt Mob -- *I was there when the floor caved in and I was and I was the one who went in the basement to see*

238

what was holding up the rafters of the floor -- it was the main gas line coming into the building.

I told Layton we had a big problem. Smoking was illegal in bars. We shut the show down and moved everybody to the Club de Wash! The visitors who were playing there let the RC mob takeover and finish the gig.

What about Club de Wash, did you work there at all and if so, same question, what were some of the shows that still stand out in your mind as being the best of the best?

I did the door at Club de around the same time I was at Ocayz, maybe a couple years after I started at Ocayz. At Club de you had to run all over the building if there was trouble at the 5 bar complex. I also worked as a cook for a little while at Café Palms.

O'Cayz = *Some of the best shows were bigger local bands like* Tar babies, Killdozer, Poopshovel, Cattle Prod, Man Clam Chow, Knuckledragger. *Later there was a 2-day benefit for the floor at Ocay'z and it was being recorded live by Ken Udell -- lots of local bands; that was cool because everyone pitched into to get that done because there were some big shows comin in.*

And shortly thereafter a semi smashed the freakin' front of the club in and we had to fit two sold out shows on stage with massive gear! And we had Sunday couch softball games with anyone who showed up and ended up going to Mazo beach if it got to hot.

Layton always oversold shows. 1 person out, 2 people in, and the guy who went out just went out to smoke. Lots of completely sold out shows and lots of Blatz beer all over!

Club de Wash = Free Hot lunch, Paul Black *hosting the blues jams,* Bush *playin' there on the first tour to about*

10 people and all of them were on the phones including me telling people to get their asses down there!!
I remember a show where ASCAP came in and shut down a sold out Peter and Lou Berryman for copyright proof and the entire club booing them out the door.

When you weren't working shows were you still hanging out at O'Cayz? Any fun times you can recount?
Most of the time I ended up working the door or bartending whenever I was there and it was always fun.

Last time you were at O'Cayz before it burned down?

It was about 2-3 years since I was at the club. After I got back from tour I went to work at the Anchor Inn on the Eastside. I brought "Tate's Blues Jam" to the Anchor Inn and pretty much moved to the Eastside.
I was amazed just seeing water in the lightbulbs in the beer cooler downstairs (O'Cayz) and sometimes wondering how the hell something doesn't blow up when we had some of the big shows there. It was an old building and always needed work but it was spliced together. We always wet down the trash at night before we closed. And the fire actually started in the comic strip. Didn't surprise me but it did really depress me because there was a lot of great memories there.

You mentioned that you also worked the door at Club de Wash. That had to be an insane experience on Friday / Saturday nights and when bands played. Can you recount any crazy moments that stand out in your mind regarding this place?

The Dwarves were notorious for being banned at clubs all over for shit they pulled with women onstage. They

240

side booked a gig while they were at Smart Studios at the Club de and I'm not sure if Tom knew because he had a date for them. But they got banned at the Club but played the Ocayz gig and I was told to stay up front and keep an eye open.

And it too burned down. Do you remember the last time you were at Club de Wash before it met its end?

Probably about 5 years prior to that day and it just seemed like there was somebody burning these places down. Rodney and Greg, the owners, were great guys and everybody there was a big family. Pretty devastating but it seemed like arson.

When O'Cayz and Club de Wash burned down, it was the end of an era. Will Madison ever see anything like these two clubs again?

Right now there's lots of people just out for the $$$ and not a lot of the "family that supports each other" vibe in the town. You don't see a lot of local bands getting those opening spots that much and thanks to the bullshit going on at the Capitol a lot of people's fun money is dried up. Mr Roberts is trying, the Knuckledown saloon is trying, Alchemy and the Wisco, and now it seems like the younger guys are booking underground shows.

I used to have big house parties with six barrels and six bands and we'd get the bands that were touring thru and pay 'em. I have been out of the loop but there is some of that going on by musicians who are helping each other out. You almost have to do it yourself!

Fast forward to present day. What are you currently doing and are you still involved with music or clubs? When did that come to an end for you?

I'm working for a (Project Home) non-profit now, 13 years, helping elderly, veterans and low income residents of Dane and Green Counties save energy and $$$ on their bills. I am putting on a benefit car/show blues show, "Blooze Krooze" to help with our emergency home repair programs that were just cut 40%!!! Also my band Jagermonster *that opened for* Tad *and did those gigs is having a reunion next week at Mr Robert... It'll never end as long as I can play music!*

Cathy Dethmers
Former Owner O'Cayz Corral
Owner High Noon Saloon

What year did you get involved with O'Cayz? How did that come about?

Cathy Dethmers: *I started bartending there while in college in 1992 because it was my favorite place in Madison to hang out. It closed down unexpectedly on New Year's Day of 1994, just as I was starting my last semester of college.*

I didn't have a solid career plan in mind, so I spent that summer writing a business plan and learning about running a business, and then opened it back up in November of 1994.

Did you book music at O'Cayz or just manage it? Who were your favorite local bands at the time?

I owned and managed the club for 6 and a half years, but only did the booking for about the last 2-3 years I had the club. Some favorite local bands at that time were Bongzilla, Cuda, Transformer Lootbag, Bugattitype 35, Pachinko, Powerwagon, Heavy Balls *and* the Flip-Offs, *and* New Recruits.

When did you buy O'Cayz? And did anyone try to talk you out of it as a bad or risky business idea?

I bought it in 1994, and no one tried to talk me out of doing it, though my parents were concerned about how it would work out since I was so young. I think they wanted me to pursue a "normal" career.

Were there any shows that that got booked at O'Cayz you regret?

I don't think I have any regrets from my time there - certainly not every show turned out as I'd hoped, but the ones that didn't were valuable learning experiences for me regardless.

Looking back on it, what were some of your favorite shows that got booked at O'Cayz?

The Cherubs, Zen Guerilla, Ed Hall, Killdozer, Shorty, Queens of the Stone Age, Unsane, Jesus Lizard, Neurosis, Old 97s, At the Drive-In.... I could go on and on!

Had O'Cayz not burned down do you think you might've modified the place? Maybe renovate it, make it bigger or would you have kept it just the same? How would you envision it today?

It's hard to say. If I really still had O'Cayz today, it's pretty likely I would have had to do some renovations over the years. It was a landlocked building, so expanding wasn't an option, but updating probably would have needed to happen to keep it viable for new audiences and bands with different expectations than what worked for a Madison club 15- 20 years ago.

Is High Noon Saloon O'Cayz but in a different location or is it its own venue with its own identity?

High Noon is a venue with its own identity, but I think it still captures some of the relaxed atmosphere that O'Cayz had.
We definitely book a wider variety of bands and events here than I did at O'Cayz, but some of that is a

response to what people in Madison want to see and do these days- so even if O'Cayz was still around, it's likely that things would have changed a bit with the booking.

What's on the property of O'Cayz today and who owns it?

The old O'Cayz property is still an empty lot, as it has been ever since the fire. I have no idea who owns it now, but I've heard it has changed hands a few times since the fire in 2001. It is strange that no one has ever built anything new there.

Do you think Madison ever had an opportunity somewhere between '94 and 2000 to become the next hip, nationally recognized music scene post Seattle?

I don't really think it did. I don't think that Madison ever had its own unique "sound" that set it apart from other cities and music scenes.
In fact, one thing I liked about the local scene during that time period was that the most popular bands all sounded totally different from one another.
Many of the shows we put together at O'Cayz during those years were a mix of genres from first band to last, and the people that came to the shows loved all of it.

What do you think it would've taken to draw attention to the Madison punk / alt music scene and turn <u>that</u> into the next Seattle back in the mid to late 90's? If not how close was Madison do you think, to enjoying that kind of national success? What eluded Madison of this?

Similar to what I said above, I think to draw that kind of national attention, Madison would have need to have a unique sound that the media could have attached a genre label to.

Though a few Madison bands from the punk/ alt music scene saw some national success (Killdozer, Pachinko, Bongzilla), I never had the sense that our scene itself was drawing much attention.

What makes Madison or *made* Madison (in your opinion) conducive to producing great local music and a great alt / punk scene? Especially what we saw back in the days of O'Cayz? It seemed like Madison had a built in audience / infrastructure regarding local music and even music in general -- promoters, fans, zine writers, radio shows, etc.

I think that because Madison has a large university, it draws people from all over the country to live here- and those people come from all kinds of different music scenes and have different musical histories.

247

So when they put bands together, there are lots of varied influences at work, and the result is really great and interesting collaborations. It also means the city has a wealth of music fans with varied backgrounds who are driven to book shows, write about shows, put on radio shows, etc.

Looking back on the Madison alt music / punk scene of the 80's and 90's, was it as strong and dynamic as you remember it or if not, how *do* you remember it?

It was definitely a strong and dynamic scene. One thing I loved about it was the strong support that musicians and music fans gave to ALL of the bands in the scene.

Night after night you'd see the same people out at the shows- they didn't come out only to see their favorite bands, but also to see their friends' bands, brand new unknown bands, side projects of other bands, etc...and also to meet and hang out with other music fans. The scene felt really open and friendly to me in those days.

O'Cayz Corral, 504 E. Wilson St., played host to a variety of rock, punk and grunge bands over the years. It burned down in a fire on New Year's Day 2001, along with the building next door housing the Comic Strip Lounge.

What's the music scene in general like today compared to back then? Better, worse….

I wouldn't call the scene today better or worse- it's just very different. Now you almost never see people come to shows to check out bands they don't already know. It's so easy for people to check out a band online first, and then maybe never make it out to the show.

I think what's lost because of this is the "wow factor" you often get when seeing a band you don't know play live- some of my favorite shows have been bands I've never heard before that just blow me away.

I also see less general camaraderie at shows these days- people seem to come to the show with their friends and stick to their small group rather than mingling and getting to know other musicians or music fans in the scene.

What's lost there is the opportunity to meet and collaborate with people who may bring something new and cool to the table. But in general, I think the scene is still thriving, and there is a lot of great local music out there. I don't expect that to die off in Madison anytime soon.

Paul Schluter
Last Crack

I remember Last Crack being a huge, huge deal when your debut album came out. How long had the band been together before the first record? All of you at that time, minus Buddo, went to high school together, right?

Don and I went to school together and knew each other since we were in the eighth grade. We weren't playing in a band together until years later but used to talk guitar all the time in school. I joined a metal band in Madison called Purgatory *and quickly brought Don in to replace the other guitarist. We moved from that band to form a band called* Hardline. Hardline *recorded a three-song demo with Butch Vig at the old Smart Studios in Madison. Don and I were both only 16 years old. Ski (Chris Havey), who eventually took over for Phil on drums in the early 2000's was our drummer in* Hardline.

We decided to move on from Hardline *and posted an ad at "Good N' Loud Music" in Madison. Phil and Todd* were playing in a band called Alliance *and answered the ad. I believe they also went to school together. We decided to join up with them and practiced about eight hours a day in Phil's Mom's basement. We all slept on the floor and woke up every day to Phil's kick drum. We were mostly playing classic rock cover songs but were also writing songs. The music for "*Shelter*" from our first album was written at that time. We auditioned a number of vocalists but no one really seemed to fit. We settled on a singer for about a year and played under the name* Monarch.

*We decided to part ways with our singer and posted an ad at the same music store looking for a singer. Buddo had an ad posted and we contacted him. We were practicing in a $50 per month storage unit (#17) and had him come out and jam with us. It was mutual appreciation. Finally someone who could really sing! He really loved how tight the band was too. I was immediately dubbed "Pablo." Todd was nicknamed "Reno." Phil became "Philo" and Don stayed Don. Our rehearsal place was named "*Sinister Funkhouse #17.*"*

Buddo brought a punching bag and hung it in the room and would punch it and write lyrics on the walls while we were putting together music. Everything from our first album was written there. I still have the boom box cassette tape demos of all of it including songs that we didn't use.

We came from a different music world from Buddo. We were more on the side of the metal music at the time and he was more into underground alternative bands. We were able to sort of meet in the middle with classic rock. We played all over Madison including Headliners, O'Cayz Corral, Shuffle Inn and even Wally Gators (the teen dance club). We were playing covers of Led Zeppelin, Black Sabbath, Van Halen, *etc. plus our own stuff.*

What is it about the Midwest being so conducive to rock N roll? It seems like the area, especially Northern IL / Southern WI really embraces its local bands.

The Midwest does really seem to love heavier music. I know modern bands like Sevendust broke through early on here with the help of WJJO. We could have really used the help of a station like that when we started. We didn't get much love from local radio. Most of the stations were either classic rock or top 40 and we didn't fit.

When "Burning Time" came out we did get some play from our friend Johnny Danger who was a DJ at the pop station Z104. He used to put us up against Boyz II Men *and other top 40 stuff in song shootouts and we would always win. He's at WJJO now and continues to support every band I've had since.*

Between Madison and Milwaukee, who had the better hard rock / metal scene and why?

Milwaukee seemed to have the better metal scene. Madison had kind of a different thing going on. Sort of a jammier, less heavy type of music, although there were some other good bands around at the time. One that I especially loved was Rapscallion *who eventually got a record contract of their own.*

How did the deal with Roadracer happen? Or was it Roadrunner then? And you guys did, what, two records for them – "Sinister Funkhouse #17" and "Burning Time." Why just two records?

We had the done a four-song demo ("The Last Crack," "Concrete Slaughterdogs," "Shelter" and "Saraboyscage") with Randy Green at Randy's Recording and were circulating it around the area. I was playing it at a party one night and a guy came up to me and asked if it was my band. He said he knew a 17 year old kid who was running a fanzine (Jake Wisely – Red Decibel Records.) in Minneapolis who talked to record companies all the time and if I gave him the tape he would send it to him.

Jake passed it along to some people and we started getting some interest from record labels and did a showcase at the Jabberwocky in Milwaukee for a label called Shatter and eventually had Monte Conner from Roadrunner / Roadracer Records fly out to see us at an absolutely packed show in Madison at a club called Bunky's. We basically were told after the show that we would be getting an offer. We signed with them when I was 19 years old, which was an absolute dream.

I really wish that we had been able to last long enough to make a third record. It would have been amazing! The growth we had from our first album "Sinister Funkhouse #17" and "Burning Time" was incredible. I believe that it would have been even more mature and we very well could have been a part of what was to become the Alternative / Grunge scene of the early 90's. I've been told many times that we were just a couple of years too early. Internal friction between Buddo and Phil plus bad guidance from one of our former managers caused Buddo to quit the band.

There were a lot of cool things starting to happen for the band. There was talk of a three month tour of Europe with Jane's Addiction (one of our favorite bands at the time). We were also hearing from our management that other bands we respected like Soundgarden, Alice In Chains and Guns n' Roses really liked our stuff. If we could only have lasted for one more album the ending to our story would be much different. It was all a magical window of time that was closed just as we were taking off.

Was the band finished by '92 or on hiatus? I know there were some issues with your lead singer Buddo and maybe conflicting viewpoints on the band's direction, etc. Can you talk about what was happening internally then?

We were finished in the fall of '91. We played our last show on tour at the Marquee in New York and had our last official show in Madison on New Year's Eve at the R&R Station.

There were a few different things going on during our tour that helped ruin us. Buddo was married at the time and eventually his wife came on tour with us, which didn't help at all.

He ended up being pretty separated from us most of the time because of that and he greatly differed from Phil in lifestyle choices. Phil was living up the wild party life while Buddo would be in the hotel room reading the Bible and going to bed early. They couldn't have been more different. We had two managers working for us and one of them was encouraging Buddo to go solo. Between all of that Buddo decided to quit the band. It wasn't anything to do with music differences though. We all loved and appreciated the music and our chemistry together musically.

In 1993 Don, Todd and I started playing together again as Last Crack *with Ski, our drummer from* Hardline. *We were still working with Gary Taylor (one half of our Last Crack management team). He helped us search the country to find a new singer. We had people fly in to audition and had two people that we thought could fit the bill. We ended up with Shawn Anthony Brown who moved his life here from North Carolina to join the band. He still lives in Madison and is one of my best friends to this day.*

We recorded our album "Runheadstartscreaming" with another great producer Brian Malouf (Queen, Michael Jackson, Pearl Jam) and did a European tour in 1994 capped off by a performance at the Dynamo Festival in Holland. We played in front of our biggest crowd ever of 40,000. By the end of the day there were over 100,000 people! We played our new stuff as well as some of the old Last Crack songs. It blew my mind to see people in the crowd singing along to Blood Brothers of the Big Black Bear!

We were hoping to get interest from a record label from that performance but it just didn't happen. When we came back from that tour we disbanded again. We were deflated because we had really expected to get something from that tour and when it didn't happen it was enough of a disappointment to just give it a rest for a while again.

A couple of years after (around 1996), Buddo, Todd, Don and I formed a band called Magic 7. *We got a lot of play from 92.1 WMAD in Madison and eventually our song "Drifter" made the playlist. I started getting calls at home from major record labels. I talked to Joel Mark who had just signed the band* Creed *and he was really interested. He's from Madison and we talked for 45 minutes. He went to bat for us and played us at a meeting but the other people that needed to sign off on it didn't like it as much as him so it didn't happen.*

In 1999 I formed my first band with former Last Crack members called Muzzy Luctin. *We recorded three albums, performed numerous record label showcases in New York and really came close to a record deal also. Monte Connor from Roadrunner really liked our stuff and pitched it at a meeting. Again, the other people just didn't see it.*

Is it fair to say that maybe your record label Roadrunner viewed the band one way and expected the band to fall in line with a more metal image which maybe Last Crack didn't fit?

Yeah, Roadrunner was very metal at the time and we really didn't fit. They were trying to put an image on us that we didn't really agree with. They tried to market Buddo as more of a madman than the poet he was.

Describe Last Crack's sound. It's kind of eclectic, is that fair? Alt-metal maybe?

Yes, very eclectic. I like the term alt-metal. I don't think we were a metal band and never liked being lumped in with that because I feel we were more diverse and were headed even more that way. We had elements of jazz, funk, classic rock and metal.

I know you and Rockford band, forchristsake, shared the same management, Gary Taylor. Were both bands good friends, tour together? Bassist Jerry Sofran has spoken very highly of Last Crack. Any memories you can share?

Yes, Gary Taylor did amazing things for the band. He had us make a list of producers that we'd like to have do our "Burning Time" album. We shot for the moon and put Dave Jerden (Jane's Addiction, Alice in Chains, Red Hot Chili Peppers) at the top of the list.
He got him for us and we were blown away! He also did great negotiating with the record label for a much better advance for our second album. He was the good guy in my mind as far as our management team went. I wish he had never partnered with the other manager who basically destroyed the band.
Jerry and the guys in forchristsake are such awesome

guys and we always felt a great brotherhood with them. I still see some of them from time to time. They should have gotten a record deal of their own. They definitely deserved it. I've liked all of the bands that they have had since. They always really kicked absolute ass live and were great guys to hang out with.

Last Crack reunited several years ago. What's the status of the band now? Are you still based out of Madison, doing periodic shows? And why reform, obviously all of you saw some kind of chemistry that was still present with the band, correct?

It's really amazing how Last Crack *just never seems to truly end. We have gotten together many times over the years and have done some really amazing things since. We have done many reunion shows over the years and always sell them out. People have flown in from all over the country and some from out of the country to see them. In 2009 we had our last show with Phil.*
He passed away a few years later. We practiced hard for it and played almost everything we had ever written. The whole show was multi-tracked and videoed and I have it all posted at www.youtube.com/pscre8tive *along with a bunch of other tour videos from back in the day. More info about that show here:*

http://www.maximumink.com/index.php/articles/perm alink/last_crack_sinister_funkhouse_reunion

In 2002 we recorded one of our reunion shows which became our live album called "Burning Funkhouse Live." Phil wasn't playing with us at the time and our old drummer Ski stepped up and absolutely kicked ass on it. He worked really hard to learn all of the little nuances of Phil's drumming which wasn't easy at all. There are a lot of little important things that have to be played to make it all work right. Phil wrote his drum parts to all of the little subtleties in my guitar riffs.

We officially reformed in 2004 (minus Phil) and recorded a four-song demo to take to SXSW (I can get you the songs if you like). We also started a full-length album of all new songs in 2005 that is still waiting on a hard drive to be finished. It was some really good stuff. I'd like to finish it sometime.

In 2005 we went back to Europe to play at the Headway Festival in Holland with Fates Warning. We even made a stop in Iceland to play two shows, which was incredibly cool. Our manager at the time was Rokker, editor and owner of Maximum Ink Music Magazine and he really helped to make all of that happen.

http://www.maximumink.com/index.php/articles/permalink/last_crack_on_the_road_in_amsterdam

http://www.maximumink.com/index.php/articles/permalink/48_hours_in_iceland_with_last_crack

Both of our studio albums were remastered and re-released about ten years ago through a company called Metal Mind. They are limited edition of 2000 copies each but I still see them around on Amazon once in a while.

Do you think Madison / Milwaukee ever had an opportunity between say, 1989 to 2000, to really become a nationally recognized scene in terms of hard rock / metal or was it just not realistic?

I think the scene around here could have been recognized nationally. The Chicago scene was strong with Alt bands like Smashing Pumpkins. I was certainly hoping for it! We just need to have a quantity of great bands happening at the same time putting out strong material. I've always felt that we all need to have a brother and sisterhood of good bands working together and supporting each other like the Seattle scene was to make it happen.

Looking back on the Madison / Milwaukee hard rock / metal music scene of the 80's even 90's, was it as strong and dynamic as you remember it or if not, how *do* you remember it?

I remember a lot of great bands that have come and

gone. I've recorded a lot of great bands over the last 20 years in my professional recording career too. It seems like the scene was better then than it is now. People went to shows more before the age of the internet.

I'll rattle off some club names and if you could give me your recollections of either playing them or hanging out at them...

TA Verns – Milwaukee

We played some shows there. One bad memory is an all ages battle of the bands that we did there. A really crappy band beat out LC in the competition by bringing all of their friends. Buddo was so pissed about it that he did a pantomime in front of the stage of him taking out his contacts, brushing his teeth and laying down on the floor to go to sleep. Unforgettable!!

Shuffle Inn – Madison

All of us (except Buddo) always wanted to play there. We got to once and had a huge blow out onstage with Buddo making fun of us (because he thought it was too corporate of a venue) and I threw a drink at him. We had a major argument in the dressing room too. Very funny to think back on it all now. I think there's some video and pics of the craziness of that night. We had another show scheduled there but the club burned down a week before our show.

Headliners – Madison

Our early breeding ground (as well as O'Cayz). We had always wanted to play there in the early days and used to pack the upstairs under age area. We opened shows for Armored Saint, Pat Travers and Manowar *there. Major acts have played there too. I'm pretty sure* The Police *and* U2 *have both played there in the early days. Loved that place!!*

Wally Gators – Madison

Last Crack's first show ever. We were called Smash Palace *and made a whopping 60 cents after expenses.*

O'Cayz – Madison

Many, many sweaty fun and crazy shows there! So many stories I can't even begin to tell. Amazing times! When we were living in Minneapolis we would still come back to play there and one time the car that Buddo was riding in to get to the show broke down on the way. He had to hitchhike to Madison and made it to the club just as we were starting the show. We had waited as long as would could and just had to start playing. He came in and ran up on stage in perfect time.

Club deWash – Madison

Last Crack 2.0 (with Shawn Anthony Brown) played there once I believe. I did get to see Smashing Pumpkins *there too. I also saw* Hum *there. Loudest show I have ever been to!*

Hard Times – Rockford

We played some shows with our forchristsake brothers there. Cool club!

On meeting bands at Dynamo:

There's a pretty funny story actually. I was working at ward Brodt Music at the time and we had Zakk Wylde in for a guitar clinic. He needed a backup band to play behind him so we got our drummer at the time and Don played bass. After the clinic he asked what we were doing and he ended up at my house.

He drank a million beers and passed out on my floor and I drove him to the airport the next morning. He gave me his home address and said to send him our music when we get it recorded. We ended up seeing him backstage at the Dynamo Festival and he was blown away. He remembered us and was kind of confused how we would be there.

It was Prong, Pride and Glory (Zakk's band), Kyuss and a bunch more bands there that I can't remember at Dynamo. That was the big show but we played other shows in Holland and Belgium also.

Above: Dynamo Fest

Above: Metropolis Fest in Holland

Above: Last Crack Burning Time pre-production with Dave Jerden at SIR rehearsal studios in LA. This is the first time I ever heard "*Man In The Box*" by Alice In Chains. Dave proudly played it for me on his Walkman and gave me the cassette tape of Facelift which we played endlessly. When we came back to Wisconsin we were all pumped up about AIC and everyone was like "*Who?*"

Above: Basic tracking for "Burning Mind" at Eldorado Studios in LA with engineer Bryan Carlstrom

Above: Eldorado Studios with Dave Jerden and the recording crew for "Burning Time"

Above: "Energy Mind" video shoot

Above: On set for the "Energy Mind" video shoot

267

Last question. Its 2015, what are you doing these days and what's the status of Last Crack?

I have a new band called Good Morning V that I really like with my long time bassist Darren Soderholm (Muzzy Luctin, Magic 7 and a tour with Last Crack). We have a singer who transplanted from Michigan named Tanner Phillips and he's an amazing songwriter, singer, guitarist. We have an extremely talented young drummer named Zach Brassington. www.goodmorningv.com

We have a video for our song "Blunderbuss" and will be releasing a four song EP later this summer and are recording a full length for release in 2016. www.youtube.com/watch?v=CI_tLhgmLKk

*Over the past 20 years I have been a producer along with still playing in bands. I even got to record the band Cold when they were in town for a show years ago. We did an acoustic version of their song "*No One*".*

Eight years ago I took over the studio that I worked at since 1996 (Sleepless Nights) and along with Darren co-own Megatone Studios www.megatonestudios.com

Last Crack will always be there waiting. Even though Phil is gone now I know it will never really end. All it takes is a phone call for an opportunity and we seem to always entertain the possibility of reuniting again for a show or maybe longer.

Dave Gregor
Morta Skuld

I was in full rock writer mode in 1990. My gig at SLAM Magazine had ended. I think I was notified by mail that the mag was being renamed and taking a different direction and I wasn't part of that new direction. I was let down but also relieved.

I decided to start my own zine. I named it after a "best of" Blue Cheer record – "*Louder than God*." The creative control was good for me. I could cover any kind of music or band without being constrained by the editors at SLAM.

LTG afforded me the opportunity to indulge myself. I covered everything from local bands to national and international death, thrash and punk bands. And the free tapes and records I received didn't hurt either.

I remember when I first contacted Roadrunner, who at that time were still Roadracer, sent me a package with 15 cassettes in it plus a contact list of rock stars who recorded for them including addresses and phone numbers. The names I remember included King Diamond, Obituary, Deicide and Atrophy although there were more I don't remember.

One of the bands I really got into at that time was Milwaukee's Morta Skuld. I saw them covered in another zine and decided to check them out myself. They were and still are an amazing band. For me personally, they epitomized what death metal was all about. So I got hold of the two demos they had available – "*Prolong the Agony*" and "*Gory Departure.*" And they were great! Lived up to and exceeded my expectations.

When it came time to contact people to include in this book Dave Gregor and Morta Skuld had to be included.

Do you think Milwaukee ever had an opportunity between '91 and 2000 to become the next nationally recognized metal scene?

I do and think it got to a certain point and then the music shifted as it normally does. And with the Metal fest it put Milwaukee on the map.

Had Morta Skuld enjoyed national success do you think it would've drawn attention to Milwaukee and turned that into the next hot metal scene perhaps?

I think not touring hurt us and the fact that we played the metal fest almost every year helped us to stay viable in the death metal scene. And with metal fest being here it made Milwaukee a hot spot for many years. And I do think it had big influence on the scene for sure.

I've been a fan of you guys going all the back to your "Prolong the Agony" demo. Why didn't it happen for you on a national level, on an MTV type scale?

The type of music we play wasn't played on MTV back in the day and we never did any videos to be played anyway. Our main label was Peaceville which we put out 3 albums on then moved to Pavement music. Right now we are working with local label Dread Records.

Tell me about Jack Koshick and Morta Skuld. I would imagine he is / was an amazing mentor / friend. How has he helped you guys and how significant / important has Jack been in the Milwaukee metal scene in your opinion?

Jack was awesome and took care of us very well. He got us a lot of shows at the Rave with the best death metal bands at that time.
He wasn't a mentor but more a manager, and he in my opinion put the fest on the map as well as the town. So he was big part of the scene and where it was going.

What drove the Milwaukee metal scene to develop as strong and influential as it did in the late 80's, early 90's? Do you think the alt / punk scene helped or influence it?

I just think all of us who were into the music scene wanted to do something cool and new and at that time death metal was new.

There were a lot of classic demos released in the scene in 1990 and that I think that paved the way for each band to feed off one another's music and energy.

Looking back on the Milwaukee metal scene of the 80's and 90's, was it as strong and dynamic as you remember it or if not, how do you remember it and how do you it see now?

It was much better back then and more fruitful, but then again I was much younger and my view on things have changed a lot since then.

But I remember a lot of shows and just tons of kids coming out and music being so much more a way of life then I do now. Now it's "Can I afford to pay the rent or car payment?" versus "let's get drunk and write a demo."

What's the scene is like today compared to back then? Better, worse…

It's not what it once was but then again a lot of us are older and have kids and families so in that aspect things are much different. But I feel it was much more dynamic and organic back then as opposed to today. I do feel the bands are really trying to make the scene bigger and a lot of bands supporting one another.

Tell me about Morta Skuld in the 90's. I remember you making a few records and then…it kind of stopped.

Well we were on fire and wrote four albums in eight years so things were great until we found out one of the band guys didn't want to tour.
That hurt us and we didn't realize it until the band was almost done. We passed up a lot of good opportunities.

When did you know it was time to end Morta Skuld? What were the events leading up to the band's demise? You formed another band after MS, right?

We went on tour and our first gig was supporting Slayer at the Eagles ballroom. Then as we got closer to our second gig our drummer had some issues and then it was known he wasn't into touring and we had to cancel everything and come home to no label no manager and no band. Sucked as we would be on the road today if things would have been different.

VIOGRESSION AND MORTA SKULD

ALL AGES
SAT. June 30th
8:00 p.m. At:
CASTALIA HALL
1904 S. 60th St.
Located on 60th and Burnham

$2.00 At the Door

BRUTALITY AT ITS BEST!

And what convinced you to reunite and give the band a second shot? What's the status of the band now?

Our old manager wanted to have the first two demos on CD and we went into studio and remastered it and then Eric Grief got us a deal with Relapse and that sparked us to get the band back together and perform. We are active and currently writing a new album with the new line up.

When you're not playing in Morta Skuld what day jobs do you guys hold down?

Nothing exciting just average jobs, factory warehouse etc.

What label are you on today, what records do you have out and are you considering touring?

We are on Dread Records *and released an EP last year. We would love to tour but it is hard with no support and we all know to tour you need money. We are doing out of state gigs this year to expand our fan base and hopefully tour next year.*

Thank you for this interview and your support and thank you to all the fans that allow us to do this and bring the music to the ears of people whom want to hear it. Cheers!

Rich Noonan
Dr. Shrinker

I'm Rich Noonan, vocalist in the band. I was one of the original members, so, I was in the band from late 1987 til early January 1991. Then the band split up. We reformed February 2013. It's worth mentioning we're only 10 months away from being together this time around as we were originally.

Give me your thoughts and recollections on the Milwaukee metal scene of the 80's / 90's:

I hear sometimes people mention how big the scene was in the late 80's and early 90's but I don't really think it got bigger until after I walked away. When I quit the band in Jan 1991 I went back to college, moved to Virginia, and didn't come back to Milwaukee until September of 1999. I was really unaware of what the scene was in all those years.

What I can tell you, is, there were a lot of cool underground local bands such as 9-1-1, Krangkorr, Speed Freaks, Cleveland Bound Death Sentence *and* Self Denial *in the late 80's. The ones you mentioned, like Realm, had a good foothold on things prior to 1989. I thought they were great and achieved some good national exposure. And* Acrophet, *I remember going to see them several times prior to Shrinker forming.*

In fact, Shrinker played CD release party / show. Since I walked away from it all in 1991 I never knew how big they got. One of my favorite bands from that era was / is Morbid Saint, *super kick ass band! They still bring it hard since their reformation. We played a few shows with them as well as Realm, forgot to mention that above. I met the guys from* Viogression *when they were recording a demo. I knew all these bands were signed to a label so it seemed like there was good momentum happening, I'm just not sure why the scene didn't explode since I stepped away from it at the time I did.*

One band that should've been huge was <u>Phantasm</u>. *In my opinion they,* Blacklist, Realm *and* Morbid Saint *were the best metal bands out of the Wisconsin area of that era. Also,* Die Kruezen *were magnificent! They've done a few short reunions in the last decade. They were a huge influence on* Voi Vod *who were a major influence on* Dr. Shrinker. *Nowadays the scene seems the same as it was in the late 80's except we're older now. We do a lot of over 21 shows and back in the day it was all under 21 shows for me.*

What kept you from becoming the next Morbid Angel or Cannibal Corpse? I thought you guys would be huge in the late 80's / 90's, can you tell me what happened?

Haha! Never have even thought to put us in the category with how big those two bands got and still are. I don't believe any of us in the band really understood what

277

attention and influence we had throughout the scene. We did well at local shows and I answered lots of worldwide fan mail but I never thought of us as much more than a local thrash / death metal band. Also we were far from mature individuals.

We were seeing other super cool death metal and other acts gets signed and we really never received any bonafide attention. Now I say that but in 1990 we had two different hopeful deals in the works that never panned out. One was with Earache, which is why we recorded "The Eponym" in mid-1990, and the other was a branch of Earache called "Necrosis Records." I don't really recall all the variables but the main Earache deal fell through because of an outside person from the label and the band kind of hosed that up. With Necrosis, I think it just never came to be.

Jack Koshick (Odd Rock Café, Eagles Club, and Milwaukee Metalfest) played a huge role not only in promoting metal but all kinds of music in Milwaukee. Any interactions with him you can tell us about?

Shrinker played shows at the Odd Rock Café. We played a majority of our shows there. A couple of the shows in 1988 / 1989 were for sure some of the best shows we did. They were just local underground gigs but they were spectacular. From what I remember Jack Koshick was businessman who ran the Odd Rock. I'm sure I was there in some form about 100 times or so over a five-year period prior to Shrinker and through 1990. Those were the days of the "all ages" shows.

Had it not been for "all ages" gigs Shrinker would've basically been unknown in the local scene besides those who bought our cassette. I got to see Death, Sacrifice *and* Agnostic Front, *three of my favorite bands ever there. I saw* Death *in the late 80's probably 6-7 times during the "Scream Bloody Gore" and "Leprosy" years, maybe once after that. When I saw* Death *at the Odd Rock, maybe 50 people in the audience total. Since we never played Metal Fest I never had any experience with him. Best show for me though was D.R.I. at the Crystal Palace.*

DR SHRINKER

What drove the Milwaukee metal scene to develop as strong and influential as it was in the 80's / 90's? Do you think the alt / punk scene helped or influenced it?

Well I can say that Dr. Shrinker started as a punk – hardcore – crossover band. I am really the one true original member. Jim Potter, the guitarist, joined a week or two later so he's original by proxy! Before Jim we cranked out probably 4-6 songs, two of them were on our first demo that we did about four months after we formed. The demo called "The Recognition," our "pre demo" demo, had a strong hardcore feel to it. That was a time when a lot of metal heads were listening to punk and crossover locally and nationally.
Some of my favorite bands at that time were D.R.I., C.O.C., Attitude Adjustment, Agnostic Front, Life Sentence and the heavily influential The Accused. *Many of my friends*

were in hardcore bands or involved in the hardcore scene. I just happened to be in a band that quickly became a thrash / death metal band. If Dr. Shrinker *had any outside (Milwaukee) influence it was because I was a huge tape trader and also promoted the heck out of the band by sending the cassette to massive amounts of fanzines and bands. Plus, as you mentioned the bands before, there was a solid representation of different types of metal from the area.*

Looking back on the Milwaukee metal scene of the 80's and 90's, was it as strong and dynamic as you remember it or if not, how do you remember it and how do you it see now?

From what I remember and what I know now I don't think myself and Shrinker really knew or appreciated what was going on here in the scene. We had no idea that the band and the scene were doing well. I think with us ending in early 1991 we probably really missed a few more heavy hitting years being active and I don't really regret it at all. I'm pretty happy with what we did and what we turned out to be over the next two decades before getting back together. Maybe the one thing I wish is that we could have played outside the local area. But we were young and broke kids so that never happened. I often wonder what it would have been like if we did it for 2-3 more years but by and large I'm glad we stopped on what I think turned out to be a high note "musically."

What's the scene like today compared to back then? Better, worse?

There are a ton more bands now, a ton more shows and much more organization now. Back then I was young, we were young and full of the unknowns and "what could be." Living the scene back then when '88-'91 is basically the meaty times of death metal is very cool to look back on now and be thankful we were a part of it. As of now the scene is cool but for me my involvement is just a hobby, a fun thing to do when not occupied by work and home life. Whatever Shrinker does and accomplishes is hopefully a positive move.

I don't think I look at the scene as a whole and compare it to anything from the past. I'll be 47 in August [2015] so I just like practicing and jamming with the band.

Then playing some shows here and there is cool. As long as it remains fun I'll still be a part of this "hobby."

Tell me about Dr. Shrinker in the 90's. It seemed like it was hit and miss. Why didn't you guys break out big?

HaHa!!! YEAH DEFINITELY HIT AND MISS! It was a hit with some headaches in 1990 but lots of good times. Then a complete miss the rest of that decade since we disbanded in January 1991. It wasn't unitl the 2000's that we had one of our older songs (from the 90's) released on a split 7" with Nun Slaughter *and also had the* "Grotesque Wedlock" *compilation released which contained the old demos. Lots of trials and tribulations.*

Late '89 / '90 our drummer was let go and our bassist who'd been with us since inception left (although he came back later that year). A real "hit" was our 1990 demo "The Eponym" which had Tony Brandt and Scott Mckillop on drums and bass; both members from my favorite Wisconsin metal band ever, "Phantasm." *Then later in the year we recorded "Our Necropsy" with the lineup I when I left. We got to play some cool local festivals in Waukesha and Milwauee. I think one was "Day of Death" and not sure what the other was called. We didn't break out big because the luck in the cards wasn't there for us in terms of label interest.*

At that point I think we started to feel a little jaded. I know I was also looking for that next step in my life of what my job / career would be. Thankfully, in retrospect, I left the band moved forward with college. The other guys in the band went into bands like "Feck," etc. When I look back I'm glad were together as long as we were and then ended. I'm pretty proud of was accomplished in the band.

And what convinced you to reunite and give the band a second shot? What's the status of the band now?

It was a longtime fan of Shrinker in a local band. He asked me if I wanted with them doing a Dr. Shrinker cover. Then Jim Potter got involved. I was hanging out with Jim for the first time in a long time since me, him and other band members went to a baseball game in 2012. I spoke to Jim about putting the band back together again. He wanted to take it slow and see what happened, just keep it low key. So, 2013, right after the Super Bowl, we had our first practice – Me, Jim, our original bassist and the guy who initially approached me to do the cover with his band, he was on drums.

About 6-7 weeks later we added Jesse Kehoe on drums. Late 2014 we added Jason Hellman (former Morta Skuld*) to the band. As for the status of the band, we're in the best shape ever. 2014 was a good year for us. We played a handful of gigs in other states. With all of us working 9-5 jobs, it's all we can do, a few gigs here and there. After playing* "Jersey Death Fest*" in October we knew we were taking a break from shows and concentrate on recording. Last few months we recorded and mixed eight songs at Howl Street Studios with Shane Hochstetler. Complete success! Next phase is mastering.*

What label are you on today, what records do you have out and are you considering touring? And what does 2015 look like for Dr. Shrinker?

Hopefully a CD release in October of 2015. Everything's on schedule now. We're doing the record on

Dread Records. *We released an old practice sessions cassette (from 1990) earlier this year on* Dread Records, *a limited release, which is basically sold out – "Contorted Dioramic Palette." It has five songs originally on "Wedding the Grotesque." One of the songs is an older song from the 1990 practiced sessions cassette called "Repulsive Habits." The artwork for the album is being done by Stephan Somers and Putrid Matt Carr.*

In October [2015] we have what I would consider a big "tour" for us -- The Thursday gig is yet to be solidified but we're playing Buffalo and Brooklyn on Friday and Saturday. Also in October we have the great honor to be doing a gig in Chicago with Autopsy *and* Midnight *and* Bones. Autopsy *is my favorite "extreme" (death) metal band ever. I've been pals with Chris Reifert for a long time, we exchanged lots of mail back in the day so it's truly a blessing to get to play a gig with them and also that he personally asked if we could and wanted to play this show.*

But for anything longer that'll never happen not because of our daily commitments but also because financially it gets too expensive to travel and do shows. Plus at my age I prefer just jamming with the band. This is really just a hobby for me and I get to do some cool stuff such as record for our first actual full length release ever and play a gig with the almighty Autopsy. We've got a couple of local shows in August / September where we get to jam with Jason Hellman on bass plus people will get to hear some brand new songs. When the CD gets released in October and we've been able to do all our gigs, it'll all be a success. Anything after that will just be icing on the cake!

Jackie Ramos
Moxy Roxx

The band's former drummer Teddy Mueller (RIP) was quite a polarizing figure, especially in the interviews he did in the last few years prior to his unfortunate death. What he was like as a band member, easy to get along with? He made a few claims that he was the reason Moxy Roxx was successful, do you agree or disagree with that?

Jackie Ramos: *Well, I couldn't answer how he was to work with. You'd have to ask Joey, Brooke or Chris that question. As far as a person, he was great. Every time I ran into Teddy he was really cool. You know, we really didn't "hang out" that often outside of the club scene, but whenever I did run into him at the clubs or at some crazy party, he was all laughs and good times.*

As far as him being the reason that Moxy was successful...There's been some rough edges when addressing this one. See the thing is, Moxy Roxx was started by myself, Chris Martinez, Mark Worple and original bassist Ron Larson.

Long story but I'll take a stab at it. I had been in a really horrible car accident on my way back from a gig in Stevens Point and was laid up for a few months in the hospital. One day Mark & Chris walked in to pay me a visit.

Here I was in the hospital, couldn't even walk, and Chris says, "Hey man, you wanna jam when you get outta here?" Off the cuff I said "yeah," but I thought he was nuts. I mean I had my teeth knocked out, my leg and ankle busted up, face split in half and this dude was asking me to jam???? I couldn't even walk dude, let alone play. WTF? Anyway when I got out, sure enough he hit me up. I was in a wheel chair at rehearsal being carried to my kit by Chris. After a couple of jams, I told them I would do it, under a couple of conditions: change the set list, and change the name.

They had been playing out under the name "Future," and I thought their set list wasn't heavy enough. They reluctantly agreed, and we shit canned a bunch of tunes from the set, replacing them with heavier stuff.

I had heard the word moxie used in old gangster movies and liked how it sounded and that it stood for having guts etc. Sitting at home one night tossing the name around, my wife at the time said, "You should add Rocks to it and have it be "Moxie Rocks." So that became Moxy Roxx cuz it looked cooler.

We started playing out as I healed and had a great following. I had done a notorious tenure with Bad Boy and a lot of those fans crossed over to the Moxy camp. After a while, I left the band to play with David Reece, but by that time Moxy Roxx had its following established.

That's the point where Teddy came aboard to play drums, Brooke joined on guitar, and Chris switched over to bass. We had recorded a couple of demos before I left, which were later released as singles after Teddy and Brooke joined the band.

I saw the single for "Time" at a record store and thought, "Wow, I wonder if they redid the tracks?" Nope. Same tracks. So that's my drumming on that single.

I eventually came back to the band after an absolutely hideous Canadian tour with Reece, and by that time some internal shit had gone down in Moxy2.0. Chris showed up at my door outta nowhere and said, "Hey, wanna come back to the band?"

Teddy and Mark had gone on to start another project. I told him, "Yeah sure man," but who the fuck is gonna sing lead? Chris and I connived to snag Joey LaVie from his current band (can't remember their name offhand).

We went to the Palms to see him play and made our way backstage during one of their breaks. Joey says, "Heeeeey, I heard you guys are gonna regroup. Who are you gonna get to replace Woerple??" I poked him in the chest with my finger and said, "You." A few months later we released the "Victims of the Night" ep and the rest I guess is Milwaukee rock history. That's the truth.

As far as Teddy being responsible for the success of Moxy Roxx...I dunno man, the snowball was already rolling. I mean whenever there's a change in a line up, people either add or detract from the chemistry. Teddy and Brooke added their chemistry and it worked but that's not to say it hadn't before that.

When I rejoined and Joey came aboard the thing took off like an aqua net bottle rocket. Was I solely responsible? Was Joey?? No. It's THE BAND. THE CHEMISTRY. THE TUNES.

I got into a small thing with Ted over the phone a few years ago after reading an interview where he said he started Moxy Roxx. I dunno man, the truth is the truth and I laid it out like it happened.

Teddy and I were cool though. I even sold him my old Artstar kit for 300 bucks when he was out in LA years later. Wish I still had it, slammin' kit.

What happened that Moxy Roxx didn't become the breakout success the band should've been? Image, music, all the pieces were in place. Any theories?

We should have moved out west, plain and simple. We flew out to LA at one point and opened for Pretty Boy Floyd at the Palace and kicked ass. We should have stayed. Huge mistake.

The thing is that at that time it was important to be where the record companies were, where the "scene" was. That and the fact that we had an investor towards the end of Moxy that got us a huge ass bus, clothes, gear etc...but the cash was coming from some shady deals and he got busted.

After all that shit we were kind of disillusioned. Actually we had come out to LA once before the Palace gig. We came out for vacation to just hang. Joey had lived in LA and said, "Man, we should all go out to LA for laughs." Next thing, we're on a plane.

While in LA we met a lady named Lucy Forbes who ran a small company called Rock Congress. She found musicians gigs. We were over at her place in Venice for dinner and I pulled her aside to ask if she could hook me up.

She said, "You gotta get outta the Midwest kid. Either LA or NYC because you're never going to make it there."

The Jabberwocky
"The Rock Palace of West Allis"
69th & Greenfield
476-5844

MONDAY	WEDNESDAY	THURSDAY	FRIDAY	SATURDAY
2 Ruby Star	4 King Pentacle	5 Trixx	6 Black Sedan	7 Centerfold
9 The Xplodoz	11 Realm	12 Unchained	13 Moxy Roxx	14 Moxy Roxx
16 Vigilante	18 A2Z	19 THE Blades	20 Raven Bitch	21 Raven Bitch
23 Moxy Roxx	25 Heir Apparent	26 Ash Can School	27 Centerfold	28 Vigilante
30 Neer				

SIGN UP NOW
BATTLE OF THE BANDS
Over **$15,000** in Cash & Prizes!

SPECIALS
Mon., Wed., Thurs. $2.50 Pitchers/ 50¢ Kamikazees
Fri. & Sat. Free Beer 8-9 p.m.

Call Trax 32
(414) 242-9010
or Jabberwocky

I sent her a video of my solo and forgot about it. A few months later a guy named Ray Brown called me. Ray made stage clothes for EVERYONE. Name an 80's band, he made their clothes. He was managing a band called "Fire" and asked me to fly out to audition. His guitar player Michael Guy (House of Lords) had seen my tape.

I ended up living at Ray's place in Westchester while I played drums for Fire. *That's how I ended up in LA. I don't think that was the original question but, whatever, haha!*

Moxy was one of a group of bands (RIPT, forchristsake, Bugsy Malone) from the Northern IL / Southern WI area that had a chance at huge, breakout success. Why do you think

290

success on a national level eluded all of you? Was it really a matter of geographic location or a shift in the music industry, etc?

Lol, see above.

"*Victims of the Night*" is amazing and on par with any music by any band out of the Sunset Strip. Were there other records or was this the only one and if so, what the hell?

Thank you for the kind words. There are demos laying around somewhere. We were going to do a full album but shit went haywire.

We had started to write tunes that were more straight ahead guitar oriented and less keyboards. Joey was on fire at that time and was cranking out a couple tunes a week.

"Armed and Dangerous" is actually on a recent movie soundtrack. I can't remember the name of it though, lol.

Did Moxy have fans in the form of major, signed bands that pulled for you, maybe went to bat for you with the record labels?

We had crazy dedicated fans, still do. The best. I don't know of any of them going to labels, but they sure were at our gigs.

Was there talk within the band of moving to Hollywood and trying to make it there?

Brooke and I talked about it. Like I said earlier, we missed the bus. Sometimes in life windows open and if you don't jump through them at the right time, they slam shut.

Moxy Roxx is still a recognizable name when it comes to

Northern IL / Southern WI music fans. For those that might not be familiar, did the band tour and did the band tour with any major, signed bands from that time?

Yeah we were on a constant tour if you will. Spent some great summers in Florida. We opened for lots of big names. Nugent, Cheap Trick *etc. Man, I swear my memory is hazy but yeah we did our share.*

We toured with Cheap Trick *all the time because we shared the same management. I could tell you stories of watching the sun come up with those guys.*

Let's fast forward. Did you ever see the end coming re: the demise of Moxy Roxx and what eventually split the band up?

Yeah. I went through a bad divorce and was kind of over being local and wanted out of the Midwest. After that drama I figured it was now or never. It was during this time that Ray Brown called me. The band also had been embarrassed after losing our bus and gear when the "investor" got pinched.

Things were slowing down fast and we started arguing internally. We stupidly kicked Chris out and when you mess with chemistry, it's over. We did a reunion a couple of years ago and both Brooke and I apologized to Chris. We fucked up.

Looking back at the Northern IL / Southern WI (including Milwaukee) hard rock / metal music scenes of the 80's and 90's, was it as strong and dynamic as you remember or not so, and why?

I think so. There were a lot of talented bands around. Raven Bitch was crazy good. I remember that time as being magic, like it would never end. I miss it, honestly. For many years it was perfect, but you can't be a big fish in a small pond forever.

Looking back on it now, do you think Northern IL / Southern WI (including Milwaukee) had any chance of becoming the next breakout hard rock metal scene say, like, The Sunset Strip was in the 80's?

Yes, if the labels had come scouting there, but it was all about the strip back then, just like it ended up being all about Seattle later. Too bad because I do believe it would have blown up.
Looking at the current hard rock / metal scenes of Northern IL / Southern WI (including Milwaukee) is as good, better or worse than how it was back in the 80's / 90's?

I have no idea. I've been living in Los Angeles for the past 27 years so I'm kind of disconnected with what's going on back there.

Who were the local bands from the Northern IL / Southern

WI (including Milwaukee) hard rock / metal music scenes of the 80's and 90's we should talk about and remember?

Raven Bitch! Haha, love those guys.

Above: Jackie Ramos (far right) with Hericane Alice.

Below are several popular venues. Please give me your thoughts and recollections about them:
T.A. Verns – Milwaukee

I really dug playing this club. The place was always packed and you had the upstairs going as well as the downstairs. What great memories.
We'd get done playing downstairs and run up for a quick drink and catch some tunes before heading out to some after party. There was a hot tub in the office there too. Cool club.

The Jabberwocky – Milwaukee

10 cent beer Monday!!!!!! We used to secretly mic the women's bathroom there. The dressing room shared a wall

294

with the chick's bathroom and we'd hang a mic up in the ceiling tiles, then run it through our monitors on stage. It was lots of laughs until some chick saw it and yelled into it, all pissed off as our intro tape was on. Haha.

Shuffle Inn – Madison

"Brat fondue at the bar..." nothing like hearing THAT between songs. This place honestly was one of the two most loved places for Moxy to play. Insane crowds, and great dressing room!

Headliners – Madison

This place was #2. Great stage, great crowds. Lots of craziness playing here.

Wally Gators – Madison

Pretty cool club. They had all ages nights there which was cool because kids would always come up to us and say, "I love you guys but we're not old enough to get in!" Now they could and it was really cool to be able to play for them

The County Line – Beloit

No memory...doesn't mean it didn't happen....

The Pier – Beloit

See above

The Loft – Freeport

See above

Hard Times – Rockford

I think I got in trouble here… (kidding -- I got in trouble everywhere…)

Any bitter feelings looking back at Moxy's career or is it all water under the bridge at this point?

No bitter feelings at all. Things happened back then that seemed so huge at the time, but really when I look back on it, it's all good. We were young and so alive man. That time was electric. I'm
very, very grateful it even happened.

Simon Wright, left, Jackie Ramos, Right

Post Moxy Roxx what are you doing today and where can we find you?

I live in SoCal with my beautiful wife Cori and our two poodles Bella and Zoey. I record with my old band mate, bassist, guitarist and writer extraordinaire Ian Mayo. We were the rhythm section for Hericane Alice, Bangalore Choir and Bad Moon Rising. *We have a project called* Deeper Than Blood.

Here's some links –

https://youtu.be/VGpqi7yIzdo

https://youtu.be/Pdvul0GwmMA

https://youtu.be/YGg4iyNkaNw

https://youtu.be/XdmtrS0fJk0

I'm also a Usui / Holy Fire Reiki Master, which has been life-changing for sure. To find out what that's all about, go to – http://www.holyfirehealer.com

I know Moxy did a reunion several years ago, any talk about getting the band back together full time or more reunion gigs?

There were some rumblings about another gig or two, and even talk about doing a show with Mark Woerple, but to be honest, I killed it.

I called Brooke and told him that I'd rather let the band die with dignity instead of doing reunions every 6 months or whatever. The last gig Moxy Roxx played was with the Scorpions at Summerfest. Leave it at that. I don't

want to eventually end up playing to 35 people because we didn't know when to say when.

I'm not going to call anyone out, but there's bands out there that play a damned reunion so many times it's laughable. I mean why do that?

I can see if you're Ozzy or something because people actually care, but if you're playing clubs and constantly putting on your Captain Past uniform eventually the thing won't button anymore you know?

So yeah, I told Brooke that I'd never play another Moxy Roxx gig again, ever. It's over. He agreed. You have to be extra careful with some things. Moxy Roxx brought a lot of joy to our fans and to us, and I would never want to taint those memories with the inability to recognize when it's over. You gotta know when to stop painting the painting.

Greg Kalember
Raven Bitch

Straight to the point with this question: What happened that Raven Bitch didn't become the breakout success the band should've been?

Greg Kalember: *It's hard to point to one single cause. For a band to really take off and have widespread success, many factors have to align exactly right.*

We were just a self-managed band with a relatively small regional following. No one in the band had any industry connections, and we didn't have enough experience to really understand how important those connections are so we weren't actively seeking them in any sort of organized, methodical way.

We were just kind of kicking around waiting to be "discovered". It was challenging enough for me just to manage the logistics of keeping a working band going while trying to graduate from high school! In order to seriously have made a run at larger success, we would have needed to focus more effort on really cultivating our original songs.

You weren't around that long but have since developed a cult following with cassette tapes you made going for a few hundred bucks on e-bay, what's going on here? I hear you get hit up all the time for interview requests re: RB quite a bit.

The EP that we made... Tear Down the Walls... has certainly taken on a life of its own. That was one of the things that we could control ourselves... that being the quality of the music we made... and we took a lot of pride in that, so it's very gratifying to me that people have discovered the record and continue to be interested in it all these years later.

Somehow the record made its way over to Europe, and there it became somewhat of a cult hit amongst 80's metal vinyl record collectors.

It got bootlegged a lot, so many people had the chance to hear it, and that sparked a lot of interest for people to own a physical copy of the EP. It's just like how music

300

goes viral on the web... only without the web! I've had people looking me up for years now asking if I have any copies left. I've sold several copies for up to 300 bucks a piece!

With all the interest in the band why not put the band back together or do an annual reunion show? Maybe a live CD or DVD...?

I don't see that ever happening. One of the things that I like best about the band is the fact that in it... I'm a teenager! I don't know if I want to mess that up. I never say never, but even from a logistical perspective it would be tough.

Did Raven Bitch have any solid label interest at the time?

Not really no. It was rumored that Megaforce heard the EP and liked it... but they had just signed Kings X and were putting their resources there. I put about 5% faith in the truthfulness of that story...

301

You guys played a ton of shows in your day around WI and IL. Did the band tour nationally or consider touring nationally?

We would have played anywhere that would have us. We were booked by Talent Associates out of Milwaukee, so we played the clubs they had a relationship with. I would say we toured regionally, going from Minneapolis down to Bloomington Ill, as far west as Omaha Nebraska and as far East as Milwaukee and Chicago.

Was there talk within the band of moving to Hollywood and trying to make it there?

Not seriously no. For the first year and a half the band was playing I was still a senior in high school. I think during that time we had enough momentum that it seemed to us like we could break out based on the exposure we were getting in the Midwest.

Let's fast forward. Did you ever see the end coming re: the demise of Raven Bitch and what eventually split the band up?

I think most of us had had our fill of playing club dates by the end of our run, so that stalled our momentum a good bit. A lot of the usual issues did the band in... chiefly financial issues. It's hard to justify the amount of work it took to keep that show on the road when you're not only not making money... but it's costing you money out of your already empty pocket year after year.

Looking back at the Northern IL / Southern WI (including Milwaukee) hard rock / metal music scenes of the 80's and 90's, was it as strong and dynamic as you remember or not so, and why?

It was a great music scene. Mostly because there were a lot of people who liked to go out and see rock shows and get crazy. When you could roll into a little farm town out in the middle of nowhere and get two hundred crazy fuckers in there who were totally into the music I'd say that was a pretty dynamic scene.

We did hundreds of shows, and I can count on one hand the number of times the bar was empty. I've played to an empty bar more times doing the few gigs I've done in recent years than I ever did in the 80's.

Do you think Northern IL / Southern WI (including Milwaukee) had any chance of becoming the next breakout hard rock metal scene say, like, The Sunset Strip was in the 80's?

I think that's a stretch. Places like LA or NY will always have the edge because they get all the best people from all over migrating there. Plus, the industry is all there. I think to make it out of a place like Wisconsin or Illinois is a challenge.

You've got to make a big noise, or get plugged in somehow to that industry, and the first thing that's going to happen is that you're going to start spending a lot of time out of the Midwest. Not that the talent level wasn't high enough, because there were some great bands around at that time for sure.

Who were the local bands from the Northern IL / Southern WI (including Milwaukee) hard rock / metal music scenes of the 80's and 90's we should talk about and remember?

I was mostly familiar with the Milwaukee bands. I still break out my Realm CD from time to time. All of the Bad Boy / Moxy Roxx/ Machine *combinations were great. Those guys were all total pros. Dan Witt's* Model Citizen *(one of his post* Raven Bitch *bands) was very strong. I produced an EP with them that I still think sounds pretty good. I liked* Firing Squad *a lot.* Mirrored Image *out of Rockford was a kick ass band.*

I'll give you some venues, please give me your thoughts and recollections about them:

304

T.A. Verns – Milwaukee

Loved the original place. Little tiny corner bar. The two level club that replaced it was awesome as well. We played there a lot.

The Jabberwocky – Milwaukee

The Jab along with Verns felt like our home base. That's where most of our hard core following was. I always wondered if we'd be the band on stage when the Jab stage finally collapsed...

Shuffle Inn – Madison

Loved the dressing room there. Felt like a rock star. Loved the sound of the stage... playing there was great because it sounded so good to me behind the kit. Never really got much of an audience there.

Headliners – Madison

Always played there on Thursday or Tuesday, but loved it anyway. Such a great stage. Opened for Saxon *and for* Blue Oyster Cult *there. Those were both great shows.*

Wally Gators – Madison

We got our best Madison crowds here. I think it was 18+

The County Line – Beloit

Always had a good time here. A friend of our family owned this place. Crowds were good.

The Pier – Beloit

I'll always think of Bob jumping off the stage during his guitar solo... sliding on his knees across the dance floor... and unplugging his guitar from his amp. It went from crazy guitar chaos to just the "clickita, clickita, clickita" of the pick on the strings. The crowd was stunned!

The Loft – Freeport

This is where Bobby tossed some dude out of our dressing room by his shirt collar and belt. Literally picked him up and threw him right out the door. The guy was in my face all pissed off because he thought I was hitting on his girlfriend. I might have hit on two girls during the band's entire run... and this night was surely not one of them.

Hard Times – Rockford

We never once played in Rockford. We couldn't get a break at any of the clubs there and I never understood why. Would have loved to play there.

Post Raven Bitch what are you doing today and where can we find you?

I've been composing and producing music for films, TV shows, commercials, websites, and theater for the past 20+ years. My company Sonic Highway Music and Sound

(www.sonichighway.com)

is based out of New York. I'm also teaching in the music technology department at the Juilliard School of Music. I do most of my composing work out of my home studio in Bethlehem PA.

Morgan Thorn
Megaton Blonde

MEGATON BLONDE

JERRY KNIGHT	MICHAEL STIX	MORGAN THORNE	MARK CALAIS	MIKKY B
Bass Guitar	Drums	L. Vocals	L. Guitar	L. Guitar

What is it about the Midwest and rock N roll? This region of the country has always, really embraced this style of music and especially the local bands that comprise each individual city's particular hard rock / metal / punk scenes.

Midwest musicians have always displayed a huge respect and admiration for their favorite musical heroes and mentors, and we relate to so much of what rock and roll stands for. There is a well-known concept called the "Midwest Work Ethic." We are hardworking, proud Americans who love music of all styles, but there's nothing like rock and metal to keep your feet tapping, fists pumping, or heads banging while you work your ass off week after week, and party equally hard on weekends with friends and musical colleagues to the tune of your favorite bands.
During the 80's, Milwaukee music clubs like T.A. Verns, Starz, and the Shark Tank became incredibly popular hubs for local musicians to hang out, party, share ideas, and check out the competition. These places were crucibles where local rock and metal were forged.

Of all the bands you've played with from Rockford, Madison and Milwaukee from back in the 80's / 90's, which ones do you remember being killer, great bands that should've made it huge but didn't?

I've always put 1000% into each and every band I've created and performed in, from every aspect of stage presence, instrumental prowess, and business management. I have amazing memories from all of them, though there are two well-known bands that were definitely worthy and deserving of record deals and prime time recognition- Megaton Blonde *and* High Treason.

Back in the 80's / 90's Milwaukee had Moxy Roxx, Bad Boy and Megaton Blonde. Plus, it also had Jack Koshick doing Milwaukee Metalfest. The city had punk, thrash and melodic metal. Why didn't Milwaukee turn into the next, say, Sunset Strip for metal in the Midwest? Why didn't Milwaukee get the national exposure it rightfully deserved?

Well, it did, but that window of opportunity was very short-lived unfortunately. Starting in the late 80's, when the bands listed above (and many others) were out there kicking ass and "touring" their guts out at every possible venue, record labels began to show up here and take notice.

Demo tapes and promotional materials were mailed out to every label in the industry, and talent agents came to the Midwest to see if these bands were anything like the hype they were generating in local and national media. Once they saw the shows, the enthusiastic crowds, and dedication to live performances that these bands were displaying, they definitely began paying attention.

These Midwest musicians had something going on; some sort of chemistry that was unique to the area and the people. Why did it stop there? I'll sum that question up better in a later response below....

Pre-show backstage antics with Marilinn Mee of Lazer 103 at the Waukesha County Exposition Center

Looking back on the Milwaukee metal scene of the 80's and 90's, was it as strong and dynamic as you remember it or if not, how do you remember it and how do you it see now?

It was fucking incredible, yes. The brotherhood of musicians, the dedicated fans, and the overall party and performance atmosphere was legion. The Midwest rocked and rolled like no other area in the US. Sure, LA was getting 99% of the attention at the time, but the talent wasn't there. The dedication wasn't there, and the work ethic wasn't there.

Amongst Midwest musicians, doing everything in their power to become the greatest bands they could, the competition was always fierce and relentless. We'd spend entire winters sequestered deep in our cold and damp basements rehearsing with our bands for days on end, riffing our fingers into nubs, bashing through multitudes of drum heads, screaming our vocal chords into oblivion, and feverishly composing the next big "hit" in our set lists. For

Midwest musicians, these weren't just bands- they were dreams.

What's the scene like today compared to back then? Better, worse….

It's complete shit, unfortunately. Ask anyone on tour these days, especially those bands who recently found their way into the all-consuming machine of the modern touring matrix. It's just not the same.

The magic that made the 80's and early 90's what they were was a very special kind of magic, and I haven't seen it since. Those who participated know exactly what I'm talking about. The vibe has completely changed.

It's not that there aren't talented and dedicated musicians out there that are eager to please, but it's much more mechanical, and lacks the kind of personal rewards that musicians used to receive for putting on the shows of their lives. I wish it were different, but the industry has mutated into something completely unrecognizable from that of the 80's and early 90's.

Megaton Blonde had everything in place. Why didn't it happen for the band on a national level, on an MTV type scale? Record labels and professional management had to be interested in the band, right?

Yes, there were a few big labels talking business with us, scouting our shows, and showing a great deal of interest. And all of the right ingredients were there to take things to the next level, except for one damning factor that was about to split the national rock/metal scene in two. That factor was the incoming grunge movement. Let me explain:

Becoming a rock star in the 80's and early 90's was not an easy journey. The bar was set extremely high in all aspects of musicianship and performance, and it couldn't be faked. People could tell who's real, and who's not; who wanted it most, and those just doing it for a taste of the rock star experience.

You had to be as sharp as a fucking katana in your held position, whether it be the guitarist, the drummer, the bassist, or especially, the vocalist. Fuck up on stage, and it will embarrass and haunt you forever. Perform with anything but your greatest aplomb, and you wouldn't have impressed the crowds, who thrived as much on the musical competition as the bands themselves. It was the complete antithesis of what was swiftly infiltrating our ranks through the grunge movement- a Trojan horse that would destroy our precious scene. Why?

Think about the band Nirvana (the first wrecking ball to punch a gaping hole into this twilight era of national rock/metal). Guys like Kurt Cobain and his ilk didn't have the type of talent nor capacity for showmanship that the Midwest rock/metal musicians of the 80's and 90's had by design, but they wanted to be rock stars so bad. So bad in fact, that they would do anything to play anywhere and for anybody just to live that "rocker" lifestyle that we earned through our blood, sweat and tears.

They didn't spend years honing their "talent" so they took what little they had and offered it as an alternative (pun intended) to the current music industry. And for whatever reason, it took. The grunge movement suddenly opened doors for thousands of musicians and wannabe performers that didn't otherwise have the firepower to compete in the existing rock/metal talent pools.

The floodgates were open, and out poured a shitload of crappy acts with guitars purposely played out of tune, mundane and amateur repetitive rhythms, anemic vocals and depressing lyrics, and an overall lackluster stage presence complete with that "I don't give a fuck" attitude.

It was the beginning of the end for the appreciation of talent and stage presence in the music industry, and it immediately stifled the pursuit of Midwest rock and roll and metal talent in the blink of an eye.

Megaton Blonde at club TA Verns

Why didn't the band move to L.A. and try to make it happen there?

The poison had already spread. LA was one of the first casualties of the grunge movement, and there were thousands of copy-cat bands contaminating the scene there, and spreading like a plague across the states to every corner of the music industry. There was nowhere to run.

Was Megaton Blonde offered any major tours to open for any major commercial metal bands of that era?

Megaton Blonde was involved in some great shows and shared the stage many with well-established bands. While not given the opportunities to travel and perform from a full time touring perspective, we played many shows with headlining national recording acts such as Cheap Trick, Winger, Warrant, XYZ, and others that had fortunately "made it." prior to the impending collapse of the scene.

Why didn't making a full length record ever happen?

It seemed that we were on the brink of a record deal with Atlantic Records when everything collapsed during the genre switch. Obviously, making a full length record is costly, and without proper label support, promotion, and distribution, it just wasn't feasible.

When did you know it was time to end Megaton Blonde? What were the events leading up to the band's demise and did you see the end coming or was it a surprise?

There were a few logical reasons that ultimately convinced me to terminate the band. The industry had unfortunately changed for the worse, and both the musical and performance style of Megaton Blonde was being methodically phased out.

At the same time, I was always thinking of ways to constantly improve the talent of each of the bands I created, and I felt that Megaton was just maxed out, both in talent and in spirit. It was a bitter end, but as a result of that decision, I soon joined forces with some other amazing Milwaukee musicians to form the new band High Treason, which was an absolutely amazing synergy of talent and musicianship.

This band went on to earn lots of respect in the local and national scene despite the rules of the game changing for the worse, and in reflection, I feel that fronting this group was one of my greatest musical accomplishments.

You went on to sing for Vicious Rumors. How did that gig come about and how long did it last?

The Vicious Rumors thing is complicated. To adequately describe my experience with the band requires a good deal of back story to explain what would ultimately become a love/hate relationship.

High Treason came to an end around 1994, after which I decided to take an extended break from the music business. About four years later, I received a call out of the blue from Geoff Thorpe of Vicious Rumors. I was a junior in college at the time, a year away from receiving my Bachelor's degree in Conservation Biology from the University of Wisconsin.

Geoff introduced himself and told me that he had heard a demo tape of High Treason's material, given to him through a mutual friend of ours in the industry. After discussing the unfortunate passing of Carl Albert, he offered to fly me to California to audition for the band. I was interested and excited for sure, having been a fan of Vicious Rumors *for many years.*

I accepted the offer and made the trip, sang my ass off during an entire weekend of rehearsals (I already knew most of their songs), and hung out and partied with the band, then back to Wisconsin for classes Monday morning. Later that week, Geoff called again and offered me the job. I was a bit surprised, and felt I had accomplished something special, but in all honesty, I wasn't ready to terminate my education for a gig that just didn't feel 100% right. To Geoff's amazement, I politely declined his offer and we said our goodbyes.

Geoff opted to sing the following "Something Burning" album by himself, not finding what he wanted in any other vocalist around the country. Almost exactly a year later, the phone rings again, and it's Geoff Thorpe. He again asks me to consider joining the band and tells me that I would be a perfect fit for their new album, yet untitled. At this time, I was working part-time for the State of Wisconsin as an employee with the Wisconsin Department of Natural Resources. I decided that an opportunity like this rarely knocks twice, and so I loaded up my Jeep Wrangler and drove to the Bay Area of San Francisco ready to make an impression.

In what would become the "CyberChrist" record, I lived and practiced with the band for several months, during which time I got to see the inner workings of Vicious Rumors in much greater detail. I began to see a very negative dynamic amongst the members of the band, facilitated primarily through Geoff's conceited style of management and how he preferred to "lead" from a very militaristic and uncomplimentary way.

It was becoming clear to me that these musicians were being manipulated and treated in such a way that there was little ownership of their positions in the band. Needless to say, I found this dynamic less than appealing, as it just wasn't the way in which I've functioned previously in my past musical endeavors.

The final weeks leading up to the recording session rehearsals were filled with friction and this eventually convinced me that this was not going to be something I'd want to continue. My final morning in California that year started with a brief but sincere discussion with Geoff on why this wouldn't be good thing for either of us, after which I was on the road back to Wisconsin, with a very stale taste in my mouth.

Thinking that I would never hear from the band ever again, about one year later, the phone rings, and its Geoff, again. He explained that he felt we both made a mistake previously, apologized for the situation, and that I was definitely the singer/songwriter he wanted in the band. After some convincing, I decided that maybe this was worth a second chance, and given that the band had acquired some serious musicians for the next album, including Atma Anur (I've always loved working with killer drummers), I decided to give this thing a second chance. These time things went much better, although the underlying tone of discontent remained throughout the band due to the way in which things were managed in many respects.

We spent about 8 weeks writing the music and lyrics for what would become the "Sadistic Symphony" album. We recorded the record at a small house studio in downtown San Francisco, and it was here that things began to quickly deteriorate once again. It was a difficult session for all, for many reasons I won't get into, but suffice it to say that I was losing interest in this band rapidly, and even through the various live shows that we performed after the album's release (including a ridiculous show in Las Vegas that

317

resembled something out of a bad garage band competition), I was ready to put this experiment behind me.

I continued to grind it out through several more shows but when word came through that we were negotiating a twenty-two country European tour complete with a step van and trailer *sarcasm* accommodations, I was ready to pull the plug on this traveling freak show. Due to several toxic scenarios in the way this band functioned and performed, I wanted nothing to do with it any longer, and I put in my resignation for the last time.

I'm proud of the songs and albums we created together, but it just wasn't something I wanted to continue. There is a reason Vicious Rumors is a perpetual revolving door of musicians. Plenty of information on that via the internet if that piques your interest.

So fast forward to the present day. Megaton Blonde has a new record out, correct? Tell us about the record and where we can find it.

A company called Retrospect Records *contacted me about remixing and releasing all of the Megaton Blonde material. Since everything was saved on 2" tape from previous recording sessions, this was an easy decision to make, and we were excited to finally have an outlet to distribute our music far and wide.*
   Some of the quality of those various mixes wasn't great, but I think Retrospect did a good job in presenting the music the way they did given the circumstances. You can find the Megaton Blonde album on the web at the Retrospect Records website (www.retrospectrecords.com) and at various media outlets, including Amazon.

And from what I hear your other band High Treason might have a record out as well.

High Treason was in discussion with the same label- Retrospect Records- about releasing all of our previously recorded material as well, but things seemed to get lost in the shuffle following the release of the Megaton Blonde album.
   The individual who owns and operates the label is a complete train wreck so I wasn't too surprised when things didn't work out. I was very hopeful we could get it done, because the songs we wrote and recorded were absolute powerhouses of emotion and brutality.
   Ultimately, all of the High Treason material remains on cassette tape, unfortunately. There are some great videos to be found of our live performances on YouTube however.

Is Megaton Blonde back together again? Who's in the band this time around?

No, there were no further attempts to reassemble the band after the release of the album. The label wanted to have the band showcase some big shows such as Rocklahoma to promote the album's release, but it wasn't a realistic goal for various reasons.

Just a few years ago, High Treason was part of a Milwaukee rock documentary called "Eternal." It featured live performances from many of the acts mentioned in this article, including High Treason, and it was a very fun and nostalgic show. For two days, local musicians and their fans traveled back in time to the 80's and 90's and made one hell of a statement- that our music will never die.

High Treason
1992

From left to right: Steve "The Lid" Mueller, Dean Arndt, Rudy Z, Morgan Thorne

Jack Koshick
Milwaukee Promoter
Metalfest

With Joe Bouchard, Albert Bouchard, Jack Koshick and Dennis Dunaway at A Taste of Minnesota 2015

How did Milwaukee Metalfest happen?

"I got the whole idea...what got me into metal in the first place was managing a band called Badfinger *in the early 80's. And our agent at the time was a guy named John Dittmar who went on to form a company called Pinnacle*

Entertainment. And John said something to me that stuck in my head, he said, "Jack, the money's in metal."

Then I started doing punk and heavy metal shows in Milwaukee and one night I had Slayer *and* Overkill, *and this was in 1984 at the Eagles club, nearly sold out, and a friend of mine who was working this show with me, Rob Ertl, said,* "You know Jack, wouldn't it be great if we could do a show with all our favorite bands?"

By that time, I'd already done maybe 40 metal shows and I thought about what he said and it was a great idea so I started working on "Metalfest," *then Rob graduated high school and went into the military but it happened in 1987, that was the first one, even though it took me about a year and a half of planning to put this thing together because it hadn't been done in America yet, I was the first.*

And I'll tell ya, the first Metalfest was magical. I didn't make a lot of money but I broke even. Now out of the Metalfests that continued, the first one made a little money, the second one lost, the third one made a little money, the fourth one lost, the fifth one made money, sixth one lost, and from seven on all the Milwaukee Metalfest were profitable.

The big ones were the late 90's / early 2000s where we had Slayer *headlining,* Megadeth *headlining, but the one that had, I think it was 1998, it had* Destruction, Sodom, Cannibal Corpse, Mercyful Fate *was on the show, Emperor, Suffocation, that was where the lineup exploded. The following year we moved it to the Milwaukee Auditorium* [Editor's Note: aka, The Mecca].

See, Metalfest had outgrown the Eagles Club at that point and the next three years were big years at The Mecca but what happened was, the city remodeled the Auditorium and eliminated the Auditorium and the three side rooms we were using and we ended up moving into the arena part which just didn't work at all, it was extremely expensive. The Auditorium became the Milwaukee Theatre after that.

Metalfest was a big part of my life, it was a labor of love. I didn't have any investors, until Metalfest VI when we moved it to the arena. I partnered with Gus Husseni who owned the Unicorn Club to do it. Prior to that, much of the bankroll came out of my pocket. The record companies did support me by buying booth space and advertising in the metal trades, though. I actually took money out of my club, the Odd Rock Café to put it into Metalfest I. The first five years of metalfest was just me. Metalfest took off when I went to work for Broadway Entertainment in 1992. Joe Balestrieri, who owned the company was a marketing genius and I learned an enormous amount from him. This took the event to the next level.

Courtesy Ian Aiken

Then Don Decker came in for Metalfest III, he was important, in fact the key guys I worked with for the next fifteen years who were highly instrumental in making Metalfest happen were Ron Goudie, Rob Grohl, Tony Trovato, Mike Fleury,

John Yorke, Barry Melloch, Joe Arneth, Marc Solheim, Bill Carlton, Shawn Barusch, Tibby Torhorst, Rob Mason, Dave London, Eric Greif, Mark Shurilla, Don Goree, Bill Bell, Chuck Meyers, John Finburg and *Brian Werner, Dawn Gleason* and *Dan DuChaine. Decker though, he was at every Metalfest from the beginning. Loved him like a little brother. He was unique, he was metal, had his finger on the underground pulse. He could spot something before it actually happened."*

Of all the Milwaukee metal bands you've worked with who stands out, any faves?

Phantasm, Realm, Morta Skuld, Acrophet, those were my favorites.

I remember several Metalfest events that featured professional wrestling.

I was working for WWE at the time as an event consultant for nine years. I just incorporated wrestling with the metal shows and had porn stars because there's a good chance that if you're into one then you're into the others as well, and they worked out fabulously. And I did it in Jersey (Metal Meltdown) for several years. The problem was, the reason we didn't continue with it, was due to venue size and we just weren't able to incorporate it into the show.

METALFEST II
LARGEST SPEED METALFEST IN NORTH AMERICA
SATURDAY, JULY 23
EAGLES CLUB BALLROOM · MILWAUKEE
FEATURING
EXODUS
FLOTSAM & JETSAM
TESTAMENT
SANCTUARY
FATES WARNING
VIOLENCE
MURPHY'S LAW
DEADLY BLESSING
ZOETROPE
SCREAMER
WRATH
EVIL DEAD
REALM
BLACK MEDALLION
ACROPHET
TIRE BUDDYS
SHOW BEGINS AT NOON
ALL AGES * ON SALE NOW!
TICKETS AVAILABLE AT ALL TICKETRON OUTLETS, EAGLES
BOX OFFICE 933-7780 OR TELETRON 1-800-843-1538
Koshick Bros. Concerts and The Underground

And you took Metalfest on the road.

I tried taking Metalfest on the road and it was probably the biggest career mistake of my life. We took it to San Bernadino CA, San Antonio TX, Clearwater Florida and South Jersey and lost $400,000 doing it, combined, and it just took the wind out of my sails. I lost $44,000 alone on Jersey. MTV2 came down and recorded that show, though.

And Tampa, see, we couldn't find a venue in Tampa proper and I made a huge mistake doing it. The whole Tampa, Clearwater, St. Pete area was at one time a hot bed for metal in the US. And a day before the event Glen Benton from Deicide asked me, "Jack, why did you come here to do this, the scene died here five years ago?" That was the "Sun N Steel" festival in Tampa and I lost $154,000 on that show.

Well, it was a hotbed for metal at one time, I mean, look at all the bands that recorded there, plus you had Morrisound Studios and for years metal bands were flocking there to record albums. Scotty Burns, who's now dropped off the face of the Earth, was the hottest record producer at the time. In fact, I had Scotty Burns and Ron Goudie mix sound at some of the Metalfest.

And Ron Goudie was Kerry King's guitar teacher. He was also the president of Restless Records and Vice President of Enigma Records. He also signed and produced the first Poison album, did the early GWAR records, Elvis Hitler, TSOL, Fear, he was basically the Scotty Burns of the West Coast. I haven't spoken to Scotty in years though, but I do talk to Ron on a regular basis. He currently lives in Amsterdam, he'll produce a record every now and then. He goes by the name of "Grandpa Death."

The reason we ended up in San Bernardino was, the venue we were at in Los Angeles, well, the owner was murdered and they closed the building like a month or two before the show, so I was out of a venue and already booking bands, and the place we were at was right across from the Staples Center, it would've been perfect but instead we *scrambled to find a place and got the Orange Pavilion in San Bernardino which was 45 miles from Los Angeles and the show tanked costing me $96,000.*

We played San Antonio and here's the thing, more heavy metal records were sold in San Antonio than any other city in America at that time and that was my logic for playing that city and we just came up short that was a $40,000 hit.

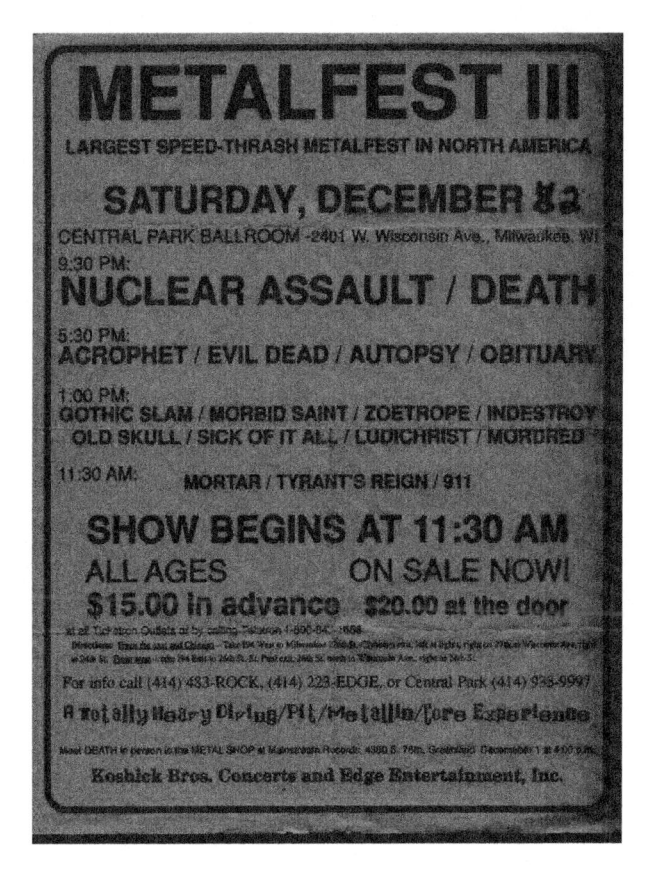

> **METALFEST III**
> LARGEST SPEED-THRASH METALFEST IN NORTH AMERICA
> **SATURDAY, DECEMBER 82**
> CENTRAL PARK BALLROOM -2401 W. Wisconsin Ave., Milwaukee, WI
> 9:30 PM:
> **NUCLEAR ASSAULT / DEATH**
> 5:30 PM:
> **ACROPHET / EVIL DEAD / AUTOPSY / OBITUARY**
> 1:00 PM:
> **GOTHIC SLAM / MORBID SAINT / ZOETROPE / INDESTROY**
> **OLD SKULL / SICK OF IT ALL / LUDICHRIST / MORDRED**
> 11:30 AM: MORTAR / TYRANT'S REIGN / 911
> **SHOW BEGINS AT 11:30 AM**
> ALL AGES   ON SALE NOW!
> **$15.00 in advance $20.00 at the door**
> For info call (414) 433-ROCK, (414) 223-EDGE, or Central Park (414) 938-5997
> A Totally Heavy Diving/Pit/Metallincore Experience
> Koshick Bros. Concerts and Edge Entertainment, Inc.

Was that loss a big reason why Metalfest ended?

Well that and everything happened in such a short period of time. My daughter became ill. I lost all of that money I mentioned by taking Metalfest on the road. Then WWE downsized in October of 2004 and I lost my job with them. I was managing Dustin Diamond, "Screech," from the TV show "Saved by the Bell" and parted company with him after a blow-up with his girlfriend. I then lost $77,000 on an Offspring, Cypress Hill show in Milwaukee and all of this happened inside of six weeks. Everything just wiped me out, it was brutal. Had it happened over the course of a year or two I could've sustained, I could've been able to handle it. It was a difficult period in my life especially when it was something I loved, loved doing.

The other thing that helped undermine Metalfest was 9/11. See, I was bringing in European acts that had never been to the states before. I was the first to bring Emperor, I was the first to bring Opeth, the first to bring Sodom, Destruction, Mayhem, a plethora of acts that had never been to the states and introduce them to the American market at either Milwaukee or Jersey and after 9/11 the immigration laws changed and it became more difficult to get work permits and immigration was scrutinizing everything.

For me to get a work permit for a band used to cost me $150 and now it's upwards of $6000-7000 and as result fewer bands were able to come over. And now they're looking at criminal records and a lot of these guys had records and they wouldn't let you in the country, even if you were arrested for drunk driving, and some of these guys had multiple offenses. Church burnings certainly don't help.

What was the story / controversy behind Manowar and the show that never got booked at the County Fairgrounds in Milwaukee?

No, no there was never any discussion of Manowar playing at the fairgrounds. Manowar played for me at the Jersey fest, they played in the main room and I had the only American appearance of Diamond Head, the original Diamond Head appearing there too.

Diamondhead was in the Theatre and Manowar was in the Asbury Park Ballroom and we over packed the room, it held 1600 people and fans were just clamoring to get in. Then we had the convention center ballroom packed with people wanting to see Manowar. That was a good fest. We had two stages. One was in a theater, the other was in a ballroom, same complex.

JACK KOSHICK PRESENTS

METAL FEST V

ALL AGES WELCOME   ALL AGES WELCOME

SEPULTURA
Sacred Reich
SICK OF IT ALL   NAPALM DEATH
BOLT THROWER   SACRIFICE   DEICIDE
CYCLONE TEMPLE   ZOETROPE
BELIEVER   ANCIENT CREATION   DISTURBED   DEVASTATION
TYPHOID MARY
DEMOLITION HAMMER   MASSACRE   MORTAR   IMPULSE MANSLAUGHTER
BRUTAL TRUTH   VEHEMENT   ORDER FROM CHAOS   CANNIBAL CORPSE   MORBID CORPSES   STYGIAN

CENTRAL PARK BALLROOM
2401 W. WISCONSIN AVE. MILWAUKEE, WI
FOR MORE INFO: 414-933-9997
RECORD PRODUCER SCOTT BURNS
$20.00 ADVANCE $25.00 DOOR
CASH ONLY AT MAINSTREAM LOCATIONS
SATURDAY, JULY 27
SELECT BOSTON STORES & RADIO DOCTORS (414) 276-4545
THE CENTRAL PARK BOX OFFICE
11:00 A.M.
OR BY MAIL: SEND A SELF ADDRESSED STAMPED ENVELOPE WITH A MONEY ORDER PAYABLE TO JACK KOSHICK PRESENTS
P.O. BOX 07422; MILWAUKEE, WI 53207

What bands have wanted to play Metalfest that you thought wouldn't be a good fit? I had heard that ex Dokken guitarist George Lynch wanted to play at one event.

Um, I'm not sure, Lynch, it's possible. Practically everybody's played it, as far as bands that have integrity. A lot of bands got discovered at Metalfest, a lot of bands cut their teeth there – Trivium, The Disturbed, Korn, Sevendust, Coal Chamber. Local bands like Realm, Acrophet got discovered there -- every year somebody got signed out of Metalfest. Dead Fly Boy got signed as a matter of fact.

I remember one year you had Riki Rachtman from MTV hosting it and Keanu Reeve's band Dogstar performing. Tell me a little more about that?

No. Riki was at Metalfest 3. Dogstar was at Metalfest 6. I called Riki, he was a friend of Shawn Barusch who put me in contact with him. Shawn was at one time the lead singer of a band called "Screamer." At that time he was host of "Headbanger's Ball" and by bringing Riki into it that year it gave us the national exposure we were looking for.

And with Keanu, a friend of mine, Jay Davis, was his guitar player, he was the one that facilitated my meeting with him. I met Keanu back in '88, he was playing street hockey back in California, he was just a teenager back then, right around the time of "Bill and Ted," his movie. We talked and we were able to make it happen with his band Dogstar but it was really Jay Davis that spearheaded that and made it happen. Keanu was a prince to work with. No ego. Very cool dude, regular guy. I've got nothing but good to say about him.

And you were manager for The Exploited. Were they difficult to handle?

Good guys, managed them for years, 1985 to 1992. The only problems I ever had with them might be damage to a room, somebody might get high and wreck some stuff, and there was damage once to a trailer and van that I had *arranged for them. That cost me a bunch of money, $6000. Kind of shitty but it comes with the territory.*

Bill Carlton, who worked with me at Metalfest, I originally met him in Nashville, he was managing a club where The Exploited did a show and the band destroyed the dressing room and I had to work a deal with him not to arrest my band but we became friends, and the band did like $1000 in damages! He eventually moved to Milwaukee and became my ASCAP rep. My nickname for him is "Gunslinger."

For the most part they were great guys, you know, I loved working with them, really enjoyed it. When we were on the road we'd all stay in the same room, I was one of the guys just a little bit older. If there was a problem, and very few actually developed, I'd step in and get us out of it.

And you managed the mighty Trouble from Chicago also.

I enjoyed managing them. I had them at Metalfest, the first one. Their biggest tour was the King Diamond tour in 1987 which Andy Somers booked. That put them on a national level.

Were you involved in negotiations between Trouble and Rubin's label when they left Metal Blade Records?

No, in fact I had just secured a very good deal with Metal Blade and didn't want them to jump. It was Rick Rubin who went to Metal Blade and bought out their contract, that's how he got them. I think I'm one of the only guys who said "No" to Rick Rubin. King is awesome! He's definitely an act I'd like to have back at the 30th anniversary show for Metalfest.

Have you ever thought about writing a book? You must have amazing stories and photos to share.

I have but I've thought, "Who'd wanna hear my story?" I've always wished I took more photos. I always thought if I took a bunch of photos back then I'd look like a poser, but man, yeah, I would have had some awesome pictures. 20-25 years where I didn't take pictures and I regret that now.

You booked some amazing shows at the Eagles Club – The W.A.S.P. / Metallica / Armored Saint gig, the Combat Tour with Venom / Slayer / Exodus, ever take any pictures of those shows?

Nope.

Did you meet those guys, talk with them, hang out?

I said "hi" to everybody. The guys I became friends with were the guys in Venom, especially Cronos, and then King Diamond also. I actually kept in touch with them for awhile. They played Metalfest. I had them booked for the San Bernadino show when I took the fest out on the road but they couldn't make it. They got caught in a flood. There was serious flooding in the Northern part of England and they couldn't make it to the airport.

Who did you manage in the 70's and early 80's?

The Esquires, *they had the hit "Get On Up,"* The 1910 Fruitgum Company, *I was working with a friend, Ray Reneri who was managing* Herman's Hermits, Gerry and the Pacemakers *and a few other British acts. Ray was Alan Freed's coffee boy, he was Judy Garland's personal assistant for five years, he was the American road manager for* The Beatles *and* The Rolling Stones, *he was the tour manager for all the British acts back in the sixties.*

333

Wasn't Badfinger stranded in Milwaukee for awhile?

Yeah they were and I got them out, helped them get back home. It was during this time that Tommy Evans and I became very close friends, in fact, Badfinger and I did four tours together. Joey Molland and I became close too. I managed them from 1982-1986.

What got you into music?

Back when I was in fifth grade there was a show at Milwaukee County Stadium called "Young America on Stage" and for two bucks me and my friend Paul Miller got to see Gary Puckett and the Union Gap. But my mom dropped me off early, at like 11 in the morning, so we walked in and the promoter told us as long "...as you don't get in the way you can sit in the grand stands."

I watched him set everything up and I thought, "...wow, so this is it?" And I saw this guy Robert Simpson walking around, he was the producer of the event and thought, "...this guy knows something." And I put it together that this is what I wanted to be. I mean, there were only three things I wanted to be and you know how kids are growing up, "I want to be policeman," "I want to be a fireman," "I want to be an Army man."

Me? A.) I wanted to get Caroline Kennedy pregnant and become a belligerent in-law in the Kennedy family. B.) A fascist dictator in some loser third world country and C.) Become a concert promoter. So I chose "C," the path of least resistance. And that's how I ended up, I started doing this in high school.

OWL with Entertainment Director Jack Koshick after their amazing performance! — With Jason Achilles Mezilis, Chris Wyse, Jack Koshick and Dan Dinsmore at A Taste of Minnesota.

Are you working with Ring of Honor wrestling now?

*Yes, I am. I'm the **ROH** promoter for Wisconsin. Been doing it now for three years. I worked at **WCW** from 1992 to 1995 on the Wisconsin shows, just Milwaukee, ever an official employee; and then 1995 I went to work for **WWE** till late 2004. I was a contract employee for **WWE**. Three years ago I came on board with **ROH**. I'm their point guy for this area, this state. And now I'm in talks with the **NWA**, the National Wrestling Alliance out of Brownsville TX. I'm looking at a large territory with them.*

Did you get to know any wrestlers outside the ring?

335

The guys I got to know and became really good friends with over the years were Al Snow, Kevin Nash, Scotty 2 Hotty, Mad Dog Vachon, Mean Gene Okerlund, Diamond Dallas Page, the list goes on.

Did you work with Bobby "The Brain" Heenan at all?

Sure I did, numerous times. Love Bobby, great guy. He's got stories. You have to read his book.

Nick Bockwinkle?

Wonderful, wonderful human being. He's a great guy and very intelligent. Unfortunately, he's starting to, being as old as he is, I think he's in his 80's now, his mind is starting to be forgetful.

Do you think Eric Bischoff gave Bockwinkle a fair shake in the WCW? It seemed like he was terribly underutilized.

Yeah, you're probably right. At that time Nick was getting up there in years also.
Any interactions with Russo or Bischoff?

I dealt with Bischoff. When I worked with Russo and Bischoff, it wasn't a lot, but yes they were in the company when I was there. I don't know, I mean, I didn't have much contact with either of the two, mainly "hi, hello, hi," but my friend Jim Cornette, who did, was not a fan of either. Jim was one of my closest friends in the company. I still talk to him. He's the one who got me into **ROH**. *Ring of Honor is growing, we're selling out shows.*

Iron Sheik, left, Jack Koshick, right

What about the infamous *"Crusher from Milwaukee,"* one of my childhood faves?

He was one of my three favorite wrestlers growing up. Crusher, Greg Gagne and Blackjack Lanza, in that order, and I got to work with Jack Lanza who was a road agent at WWE. So I worked with Jack for nine years, we actually became pretty good friends. Mad Dog Vachon I got to know afterwards and became very close to also.

Crusher became one of my closest friends, in fact I was a pall bearer at his funeral. I was with him the night before he went into the hospital and then, well, he never came out. In fact, that night we went out to a buffet at the casino, because he really liked it, and then after looked for a place to do karaoke because he enjoyed singing "Roll out the Barrel."

I remember we went to this bar and some guy at the other end of the bar was giving the lady bartender a problem. They didn't have Crusher's song "Roll out the Barrel" so he didn't sing, but this guy with spiked hair and piercings all over who was giving this girl a hard time, Crusher who was 79, and very old school, leaned over to me and said, "You know Jack, I've never lost a bar fight!" {Laughs}.

You know, I went over to his house one time and he was bench pressing 315 pounds at 79 years old, he goes, "Jack, spot me." I said "Crush I don't know about this." He loved to work out. Since his wife passed away, he wasn't the same guy after though.

It's wrestling legend that Crusher would smoke cigars and drink beer before a match.

Oh sure. Crusher used to train by taking a quarter barrel on each shoulder and running down the lakefront. Crush might've been the first American to clean and jerk 500 pounds. He had 24" arms, 54" chest, 21" neck and those were 20 megaton biceps, I tell ya.

Are you still promoting rock concerts or is it strictly wrestling these days?

I'm sort of a hired gun. I just did Night Ranger *and* Quiet Riot *in Omaha. We've got* Warrant *and* Great White *in Omaha coming up. I book fairs and festivals around the country. I've got a bunch of things going on right now. About 20-30 events a year, a far cry from the 300 shows I did a year. 1986-2000 I was doing 300 shows a year. In my career I've done over 5000 shows total. Here's something to think about: 1 out of 10 new promoters makes it to show number 3. And only 1 out of 10 will make it show number 10. The mortality rate of concert promoters is huge.*

Have you thought about resurrecting Metalfest?

I have and if I do it, it'll be in 2017 for the 30th anniversary.

Would it be back at the Eagles Club?

I haven't talked to them but I'm not ruling it out. Problem is, I ran that venue for nine years and when I left and took Metalfest, we had a falling out. I'm thinking Waukesha Expo right now. But, my vision is something more in line with like Wacken, open air, 2-3 days, Friday – Sunday maybe, Waukesha fairgrounds where you can do camping. Eddie Trunk has been to my shows before, I could see him

MC'ing, Lonn Friend also. I've had Chuck Billy, Niko McBrain, King Diamond MC'ing past shows...

That was the sight of the last Metalfest. Looking back on it, what's your opinion of it?

You know... {Sighs}.... I don't know how we got through it. We had issues with one of the PA systems, something blew and caused a lot of technical issues. One of our radio station sponsors supplied sound and lights at that stage and, well, it caused a lot of headaches for me. This time would be different. It'd be held outside with a major headliner.

Aside from the last Metalfest, any regrets with it?

Regrets? I never would've taken it on the road. Jersey was good, I should've kept in Milwaukee and New Jersey. And I probably wouldn't have left the Eagles Club. When I left I basically severed ties as a promoter in that building. Had an office there from 1992 to 1999.

FINIS

About the Author:

Theron Moore has been freelance writing since 1989. He's contributed articles to SLAM Magazine (Stateline Area Magazine, Northern IL / Southern WI), Sheet Metal Magazine and has published two zines -- *Louder Than God* and *The Saint Vitus Press & Poetry Review*.

He's had poetry published by *Red Fez* (web site), *Poetry Motel* (web site), *Poesy Magazine*, *Tree Killer Ink*, *Criminal Class Review* and *The Saint Vitus Press & Poetry Review*.

He's contributed music / movie reviews / interviews to websites *horrornews.net*, *Wormwood Chronicles*, *The Sludgelord* and edits his own webzine *Church of the Necronomicon*.

In 2011 he edited and published his first book, Gangsters, Harlots and Thieves: Down and out at the Hotel Clifton. He did the layout and editing for Rockford Area Music History Part I by Todd Houston. Both titles are available on Amazon and Createspace.

Moore has the following books soon to be published 2015 / 2016:

Blood on the Screen, Blood on the Page: *The Influence of Cinema on Outlaw Poetry.*

The Small Press Revolution, 1975 to Present: *An Inside Look at the Writers who lived it.*

Photo / Image Credits:

All photos used by permission of the bands and / or individuals in this book; all photos were found on the World Wide Web and / or Facebook pages. Other exceptions are noted and documented. The author of this book claims no copyright, ownership, legal or otherwise, unless specifically stated.

Slam Magazine images from the collection of Theron Moore

Louder Than God images from the collection of Theron Moore

Photos / images used in Bun E Carlos interview used courtesy of Bun E Carlos Facebook Page

Image Cheap Trick flyer used in Bun E. Carlos interview from the collection of Theron Moore

Photos used in Mark Snodgrass interview used courtesy of Mark Snodgrass Facebook Page

Photos / images used in Greg C interview provided by / used courtesy of Greg C.

Gig flyers used in Greg C interview from the collection of Theron Moore

Photos and images in Brian Carter interview used courtesy of Brian Carter Facebook Page and Brian Carter

Live stills of Sarkoma performing in Brian Carter interview from YouTube video, "Sarkoma (paper) 1993 Cherryvale Mall Rockford, IL." Uploaded by Brian Carter. https://www.youtube.com/watch?v=AZ6LBwYJS0c

Photos / images used in Glenn Rene Zeringue Junior used courtesy of Bludgeoned Nun Facebook Page

Photos / images of Pinewood Box used in Dan Gildea interview courtesy of Dan Gildea

Photos / images of Pinewood Box used in Dave Ensminger interview courtesy of Pinewood Box Facebook Page

Images of Dave Ensminger's books, Visual Vitriol and Left of the Dial from Amazon.com - Other images courtesy Dave Ensminger Facebbok Page

Photos / images used in Jerry Sofran interview courtesy of forchristsake and Jerry Sofran Facebook Page

Photos / images used in Ray Horstheimer interview courtesy of Ray Horstheimer Facebook Page

Photos / images used in Paul Bronson interview / Midwest Jamfest segment courtesy of Zanthus Facebook Page

Photos / images used in Dave Potter interview courtesy of Dave Potter Facebook Page

Midwest Jamfest Poster, gig review and backstage pass, from the collection of Mossy Vaughn.

Photos / images used in Todd Houston interview courtesy of Todd Houston Facebook Page

Photos / images used in Greg DeCarlo interview courtesy of Greg DeCarlo Facebook Page. "Reflections" gig flyer courtesy of Todd Houston / Rockford Area Bands Nostalgia Facebook Page.

Photos / images used in Steve Moriarity interview courtesy of Steve Moriarity Facebook Page

Photos / images used in Mike Korn interview courtesy of Mike Korn Facebook Page

Images of Wormwood Chronicles used in Mike Korn interview courtesy of Pinewood Box Facebook Page

Photos used in "Madison and Milwaukee" from the collection of Theron Moore except where noted.

Image of Battalion of Saints / Imminent gig flyer used in Robert Corbit interview courtesy of Imminent Attack website: http://imminentattack.com/

Photos / images used in Brad Skaife interview courtesy of Imminent Attack website: http://imminentattack.com/

Photos / images used in Bill Feeny interview courtesy of Appliances SFB Facebook Page

Photos / images used in interview with Dan Hobson interview courtesy of Killdozer Facebook Page

Photos / images used in interview with Mike Turnis courtesy of Mike Turnis

Photos / images used in interview with Blunt Rapture courtesy of Blunt Rapture. Other: World Wide Web.

Photos used in interview with Bucky Pope courtesy of Bucky Pope and his Facebook Page

Black and white photo of O'Cayz Coral found on the World Wide Web. Credit: Unknown.

Small Factory gig flyer, page 233, collection of Theron Moore

Vulgar Boatmen gig flyer, page

Photos / images used in Cathy Dethmers interview courtesy of Cathy Dethmers Facebook Page; http://host.madison.com/o-cayz-corral/image_123ced63-1644-5139-8360-027388347efc.html#ixzz3eoVYxkby; Wisconsin State Journal. 1/1/02. Image: D.j. El Serpentine, https://www.facebook.com/groups/199264986843318/

345

Photos / images used in Paul Schluter interview courtesy of Paul Schluter

Photos / images used in Dave Gregor interview courtesy of Morta Skuld Facebook Page

Photos / images used in Rich Noonan interview courtesy of Dr Shrinker Facebook Page

Photos used in Jackie Ramos interview courtesy of Jackie Ramos / Moxy Roxx Facebook Page

Photos / images used in Greg Kalember interview courtesy of Raven Bitch Facebook Page / Raven Bitch website: http://www.ravenbitch.com/RavenBitch/Home.html

Photos / images used in Morgan Thorn interview courtesy of Megaton Blonde Facebook Page. High Treason photo courtesy of world wide web

Photos / images with Jack Koshick courtesy of Jack Koshick Facebook Page

Photos / images used in Jack Koshick interview courtesy of the World Wide Web, Paul Schluter and the collection of Theron Moore